WWW.AVALONHILLS.ORG

Avalon Hills

RESIDENTIAL EATING

DISORDERS PROGRAM

800-330-0490

AVALON HILLS HEALTH CARE, INC.	AVALON HILLS HEALTH CARE, INC.
ADULT FACILITY	ADOLESCENT FACILITY
8530 SOUTH 500 WEST	7852 WEST 600 NORTH
PARADISE, UT 84328	PETERSBORO, UT 84325
TEL: (435) 245-4537	TEL: (435) 753-3686

EATING DISORDERS CLINICAL POCKET GUIDE

EATING DISORDERS CLINICAL POCKET GUIDE

Introduction to The Eating Disorders Clinical Pocket Guide

This book is intended for healthcare providers in any discipline who interact with men, women, children, or adolescents who have known or suspected eating disorders. Because eating disorders are wrongly considered rare in many educational programs, professional medical and behavioral training is often not adequate preparation for the realities of providing care to malnourished or mentally unwell patients. Because of the wrongful stigma often associated with eating disorders in some cultures, many healthcare providers are currently working with patients or clients who appear deceptively healthy while concealing potentially life-threatening eating behaviors and related physical symptoms. This book is intended to provide guidance and information to healthcare providers in any field who wish to provide better, more appropriate, and timely care.

Please note: This book is not intended to diagnose or treat any disease or to be a replacement for medical, behavioral, or mental health care. This book is a guide for health professionals and must be used in conjunction with professional expertise and clinical judgment. If you suspect you or someone you know has an eating disorder, or if you are experiencing symptoms of an eating disorder or any other medical condition, please seek appropriate professional care.

Eating disorders are psychiatric disorders classified as "process addictions," i.e. behaviors that serve a soothing purpose to stress-related brain chemical imbalances.

As opposed to being completely biologically based, as in cystic fibrosis, or completely environmental, as in food poisoning, eating disorders are most likely a fusion of a biological component that causes sensitivity to environmental factors. This sensitivity, as yet unnamed, may cause eating and related behaviors (purging, exercise, etc.) to be more rewarding to susceptible individuals. When under stress, whether emotional or situational, these sensitive brains benefit from the chemical changes induced by these behaviors.

While binge eating, self-induced vomiting, excessive exercise, and starvation may appear self-destructive to outside observers, the person practicing these behaviors is using them to stay alive. Many individuals with eating disorders find themselves able to see both sides of their disorder; the benefits as well as the destruction. Usually this awareness is not enough to eradicate the behaviors, since a sensitive person, especially one who is not aware of other options, may be as addicted to dysfunctional eating behaviors as a person abusing drugs. This is why psychiatric medications are often needed to break the cycle of destructive behaviors, and behavioral counseling must be added to provide other options to vent confusing or uncomfortable feelings. In addition, eating disorder treatment must include nutritional rehabilitation, if a patient is malnourished, and nutritional education and counseling to support new and continued health-promoting eating.

A calorie-restricted diet is the most commonly reported triggering event for eating disorders, whether intended or not to produce weight loss. Many patients began their eating disorders after initially losing weight on purpose, and then discovering that a svelter shape does not protect them from all the negative feelings they associated with their former weight or size. This caused the mistaken belief that further weight loss was needed.

For other patients, an acute illness or other cause of unintentional weight loss (e.g. jaw surgery, painful orthodontia, anxiety) produced the same beneficial brain chemistry as intentional weight loss through dieting. When the accidental weight loss was socially reinforced (e.g. "You look great! How'd you do it?"), the desire to remain at this weight prompted continuation of restrictive eating habits or adoption of unhealthy weight control practices.

Because of the brain chemical changes accompanying stress, and the relief that is felt while manipulating food, eating disorders can be triggered by any event that exceeds an individual's ability to cope, whether objectively or subjectively positive or negative. In traditional education, students are not taught social skills, and children who are academically or athletically advanced or delayed may feel "left out," "different," or "not (something) enough." If they attribute these uncomfortable feelings to weight or shape differences, and especially if this is supported by comments from family members or other adults, dieting may be the chosen method to feel better.

While dieting and associated weight loss work temporarily, providing the dual pleasures of social affirmation and brain chemistry relief, as with other addictions, more extreme practices are ultimately needed to produce the same results. Patients who initially skip one meal are ultimately fasting all day. Patients who occasionally overeat in secret are ultimately binge eating and vomiting on a daily basis. Feeling ashamed of their increasingly uncontrollable behavior, many tell no one their problems, as they are afraid to be judged or shamed by family, friends, and even health professionals.

This fear is often justified, as I have heard eating disorders pejoratively described as "attention-seeking," "disgusting," or "a way to get back" at someone. To the contrary, most of my patients report initiating their behaviors for what seemed to be a positive reason, but the increased attention they received (whether positive, in the form of social approval, or negative, in the form of increased family anger) fueled continuation of the disorder. In fact, many patients are actively trying to fight their disorder and yet cannot consciously control their behaviors.

In addition, many individuals not meeting criteria for an eating disorder at all continue to struggle with less than adequate nutrition status, due to reliance on unhealthy practices to maintain desired health or weight. I find it ironic that many of the food delusions described by patients with eating disorders are the very same myths that diet providers propound as sensible weight loss techniques.

I believe that most of my patients are perfectly sane, just very confused; they are simply trying to follow the conflicting directions our society delineates as necessary for social acceptance, and the confusion that results makes healthy and rational decision-making impossible.

Our society reinforces these "crazy-making" decisions by sending pervasive messages that promote achieving success through both unhealthy eating practices and unhealthy weight control practices. We are told to consume all manner of questionably prepared and processed foods and beverages, in order to be "cool," accepted, attractive, and "good." We are also provided with countless options to negate the effects of these products – diarrhea pills, calorie-free liquid chemicals, eating disordered diet programs, organ mutilating surgeries – all packaged in a manner that we don't even notice how incompatible with life they are.

At the same time that we are bombarded with products, we are bombarded with the message that we are not trying hard enough… we must not be, because if we were, we would be problem and blemish-free. If we had achieved our goals of being cool, accepted, attractive, and good, we would have no problems, no bad moods, no negative feelings, no boredom. Since trying to eliminate all of the above is equivalent to overhauling the human condition, we are never successful, yet we continue to strive for the magical cure that will "fix" us and make us "enough."

The one solution that is rarely heard above the clamor of consumption is the basic premise that we are already "good enough." That acceptance of who and where we are is truly the only way to lasting self-care and ultimate change. This seeming contradiction is absolutely simple to understand if one believes that "You" and your body are two separate entities. You are the part who is perfect as is; your body is simply your physical space. Sometimes behaviors that help You survive are harmful to your body, and sometimes things you do to "improve" your body are quite dangerous to the rest of You.

This premise, though very acceptable, if not essential, in many religions and scientific disciplines, for some reason remains difficult to blend with modern life. The final frontier in eating disorders care is an acceptance of the inner self as a component of wellness and sickness. We must in some way convey to our patients that they are not the sum of their body parts. Otherwise they will continue to try to change their bodies when they really need to change their minds.

Someday I presume future health professionals will look at this book and shake their heads. "How simple," they will think, "how basic the information they had back then. Amazing they cured as many as they did." We are on the brink of more sophisticated brain imaging, more specific genetic testing, and a more intentional society. The more we recognize eating disorders and other addictions and mental health issues as the symptoms of a sick society instead of the character flaws of weak individuals, the more we will shatter the stigma, recognize that we are all suffering, and make giant leaps in the management, treatment and hopefully cure of all of the impediments to mental health and wellness. As a tool to help us on this path, I give you The Eating Disorders Pocket Guide. Jessica Setnick, MS, RD/LD

Diagnosing Eating Disorders

On the following pages you will find the officially recognized diagnostic criteria for only three eating disorders. I suspect there are more, although medical science at this time does not differentiate between them. Right now we use symptoms to determine disorders, and in the case of eating disorders, this doesn't seem to be adequate. Many patients with similar symptoms describe very different underlying issues, disease progression, and treatment side effects.

Diagnoses have been standardized to facilitate research and treatment, but especially in the case of eating disorders, they may not represent the true experience of any one person. Thankfully, the diagnosis of Eating Disorder, Not Otherwise Specified, can be applied as needed when the traditional diagnoses of Anorexia Nervosa and Bulimia Nervosa are not adequate to describe a particular patient's symptoms.

In recent years, the diagnosis of Binge Eating Disorder has been proposed as a singular disorder rather than a byproduct of bulimia. Preliminary research has suggested that as many as half of all individuals seeking medical care for weight loss meet the criteria for this disorder. It is unfortunate that many so-called "weight loss" programs, regardless of method, do not appear to screen for emotional issues or even mental health, before enrolling participants.

For eating disordered individuals, weight loss "advice" in the absence of mental health care can be at a minimum inadequate, possibly unethical, and in some cases, dangerous. Diagnosing eating disorders is a difficult business. If it is part of your duties, please consider the effects that a "label" can have on a person who is struggling to self-identify.

Diagnoses are appropriate for medical charts and insurance forms, not as a manner of describing human beings. Patients should be discouraged from identifying themselves as "anorexic" or "bulimic," and should practice using their names and other descriptive terms, such as "I am recovering from anorexia" or "I struggle with bulimia."

When diagnosing patients, keep in mind that eating disorders can be disguised as a variety of other ailments, including depression, gastrointestinal diseases, hormone and/or menstrual abnormalities, and "I'm just normally this weight. I must have a fast/slow metabolism." Conversely, patients have been wrongly been told they have eating disorders when they are instead suffering from one of the diagnoses mentioned above. Sometimes only time will tell the etiology of what present as disordered eating behaviors.

Often physical symptoms actually predate disordered eating behaviors, and sorting this out becomes a chicken-egg conundrum with no solution. The key is to provide appropriate treatment for discernible symptoms, and then additional treatment as needed for persistent symptoms or new symptoms that arise.

Also important to note, is that body weight in itself is no better criteria for diagnosing an eating disorder than body height. Correct diagnosis requires additional information, such as weight history, eating practices, nutrition beliefs, and more. A comprehensive eating disorder evaluation should allow time for the adequate assessment of patients after medical stabilization and prior to behavioral treatment, since generic nutrition advice poorly matched to a patient's needs can potentially make an eating disorder significantly worse. Prior to making dietary recommendations, a full assessment of current behaviors, beliefs, and eating habits is needed, as opposed to the current despicable trend that can be summarized as "diet and exercise cure everything."

For example, if a patient presents as overweight, with high cholesterol, insomnia, hypertension, depression and joint pain, immediate treatment should address cholesterol, sleep, depression, blood pressure, and pain. If another patient presents complaining of nightly binge eating, with high cholesterol, insomnia, hypertension, depression and joint pain, immediate treatment should be exactly the same. Do not assume that eating is the root of the problems. Perhaps the depression caused the eating, or the pain, or the insomnia. Or a small weight gain may have caused insomnia, which caused night eating, which caused further weight gain. A thorough eating and weight history assessment is necessary, once health parameters are under control. Only then should physical activity and eating be addressed as possibilities to promote long-term and possibly non-pharmaceutical relief.

DSM-IV Criteria for Anorexia Nervosa (307.1)

Criterion	Description
A	Refusal to maintain body weight at or above a minimally normal weight for age and height (e.g., weight loss leading to maintenance of body weight less than 85% of that expected or failure to make expected weight gain during period of growth, leading to body weight less than 85% of that expected).
B	Intense fear of gaining weight or becoming fat, even though underweight.
C	Disturbance in the way in which one's body weight or shape is experienced, undue influence of body weight or shape on self-evaluation, or denial of the seriousness of the current low body weight.
D	In postmenarcheal females, amenorrhea, i.e., the absence of at least three consecutive menstrual cycles. (A woman is considered to have amenorrhea if her periods occur only following hormone, e.g., estrogen, administration.)
Specify type	
Restricting type	During the current episode of anorexia nervosa, the person has not regularly engaged in binge-eating or purging behavior (i.e., self-induced vomiting or the misuse of laxatives, diuretics, or enemas).
Binge-eating/ purging type	During the current episode of anorexia nervosa, the person has regularly engaged in a binge-eating or purging behavior (i.e., self-induced vomiting or the misuse of laxatives, diuretics, or enemas).

Source: American Psychiatric Association. Reprinted with permission from the Diagnostic and Statistical Manual of Mental Disorders, Fourth Edition, Text Revision, Copyright 2000.

DSM-IV Criteria for Bulimia Nervosa (307.51)

Criterion	Description
A	Recurrent episodes of binge eating, characterized by both of the following:
	(1) Eating, in a discrete period of time (e.g., within any 2-hour period), an amount of food that is definitely larger than most people would eat during a similar period of time and under similar circumstances.
	(2) A sense of lack of control over eating during the episode (e.g., a feeling that one cannot stop eating or control what or how much one is eating).
B	Recurrent inappropriate compensatory behavior in order to prevent weight gain, such as self-induced vomiting; misuse of laxatives, diuretics, enemas, or other medications; fasting; or excessive exercise.
C	The binge eating and inappropriate compensatory behaviors both occur, on average, at least twice a week for 3 months.
D	Self-evaluation is unduly influenced by body shape and weight.
E	The disturbance does not occur exclusively during episodes of anorexia nervosa.
Specify type	
Purging type	During the current episode of bulimia nervosa, the person has regularly engaged in self-induced vomiting or the misuse of laxatives, diuretics, or enemas.
Nonpurging type	During the current episode of bulimia nervosa, the person has used other inappropriate compensatory behaviors, such as fasting or excessive exercise, but has not regularly engaged in self-induced vomiting or the misuse of laxatives, diuretics, or enemas.

Source: American Psychiatric Association. Reprinted with permission from the Diagnostic and Statistical Manual of Mental Disorders, Fourth Edition, Text Revision, Copyright 2000.

DSM-IV Research Criteria for Binge-Eating Disorder

Criterion	Description
A	Recurrent episodes of binge eating, characterized by both of the following:
	(1) Eating, in a discrete period of time (e.g., within any 2-hour period), an amount of food that is definitely larger than most people would eat during a similar period of time and under similar circumstances.
	(2) A sense of lack of control over eating during the episode (e.g., a feeling that one cannot stop eating or control what or how much one is eating).
B	The binge-eating episodes are associated with three (or more) of the following:
	(1) eating much more rapidly than normal
	(2) eating until feeling uncomfortably full
	(3) eating large amounts of food when not feeling physically hungry
	(4) eating alone because of being embarrassed by how much one is eating
	(5) feeling disgusted with oneself, depressed, or very guilty after overeating
C	Marked distress regarding binge eating is present.
D	The binge eating occurs, on average, at least 2 days a week for 6 months.
E	The binge is not associated with the regular use of inappropriate compensatory behaviors (e.g. purging, fasting, excessive exercise) and does not occur exclusively during the course of Anorexia Nervosa or Bulimia Nervosa.

Source: American Psychiatric Association. Reprinted with permission from the Diagnostic and Statistical Manual of Mental Disorders, Fourth Edition, Text Revision, Copyright 2000.

DSM-IV Criteria for Eating Disorder NOS (307.50)

The Eating Disorder Not Otherwise Specified category is for disorders of eating that do not meet the criteria for any specific Eating Disorder. Examples include:

1. For females, all of the criteria for Anorexia Nervosa are met except that the individual has regular menses.
2. All of the criteria for Anorexia Nervosa are met except that, despite significant weight loss, the individual's current weight is in the normal range.
3. All of the criteria for Bulimia Nervosa are met except that the binge eating and inappropriate compensatory mechanisms occur at a frequency of less than twice a week or for a duration of less than 3 months.
4. The regular use of inappropriate compensatory behavior by an individual of normal body weight after eating small amounts of food (e.g. self-induced vomiting after the consumption of two cookies).
5. Repeatedly chewing and spitting out, but not swallowing, large amounts of food.
6. Binge-eating disorder: recurrent episodes of binge eating in the absence of the regular use of inappropriate compensatory behaviors characteristic of Bulimia Nervosa (see above for suggested research criteria).

Source: American Psychiatric Association. Reprinted with permission from the Diagnostic and Statistical Manual of Mental Disorders, Fourth Edition, Text Revision. Copyright 2000.

Related ICD-9 Diagnosis Codes

Abnormal Weight Loss 783.21

Amenorrhea 626.0

Anorexia Nervosa 307.1

Anxiety Disorder NOS 300.0

Body Dysmorphic Disorder 300.7

Borderline Personality
Disorder 301.83

Bulimia Nervosa 307.51

Constipation 564.0

Conversion Disorder 300.11

Diarrhea 558.9

Eating Disorder NOS 307.50

Feeding Disorder of Infancy or Early
Childhood 307.59

Hypercholesterolemia 272.0

Hyperlipidemia 272.3

Hypertension, Essential 401.9

Hypoglycemia 251.2

Malnutrition,
Mild Degree 263.1
Moderate Degree 263.0

Nutritional Deficiency 269.9

Obesity 278.0

Obsessive-Compulsive
Disorder 300.3

Pica 307.52

Rumination Disorder 307.53

Vitamin Deficiency 269.2

Source: International Classification of Diseases 9th Revision, U.S. Department of Health and Human Services, Centers for Disease Control and Prevention, National Center for Health Statistics, Hyattsville, MD, 20782.

Standardized Screening Tools for Eating Disorders

Name	Form	Description	Reference(s)
Diagnostic Survey for Eating Disorders (DSED)	Can be used as self-report or semi structured interview	Twelve sections cover demographics, weight history and body image, dieting, binge eating, purging, exercise, related behaviors, sexual functioning, menstruation, medical and psychiatric history, life adjustment, and family history	Johnson C: Diagnostic Survey for Eating Disorders (DSED), in The Etiology and Treatment of Bulimia Nervosa. Edited by Johnson C, Connors M. New York, Basic Books, 1987
Eating Attitudes Test	Self-report	Brief (26-item), standardized, self-report screening test of symptoms and concerns characteristic of eating disorders; completion time: 5-10 minutes	Garner DM, Olmsted MP, Bohr Y, Garfinkel PE: The Eating Attitudes Test: psychometric features and clinical correlates. Psychol Med 1982; 12:871-878Garner DM: Psychoeducational principles in the treatment of eating disorders, in Handbook for Treatment of Eating Disorders. Edited by Garner DM, Garfinkel PE. New York, Guilford Press, 1997, pp 145-177
Eating Disorders Examination (EDE)	Semi structured interview	Measures the presence and severity of eating disorder features and provides operational DSM-IV diagnoses	Fairburn CG, Cooper Z: The Eating Disorders Examination -12th ed, in Binge Eating: Nature, Assessment and Treatment. Edited by Fairburn CG, Wilson GT. New York, Guilford Press, 1993
EDE-Q4	Self-report	Self-report version of the EDE, designed for situations in which an interview cannot be used; validated against the EDE	Fairburn CG, Beglin SJ: The assessment of eating disorders: interview or self-report questionnaire? Int J Eat Disord 1994; 16:363-370

(continued)

Standardized Screening Tools for Eating Disorders
(continued)

Name	Form	Description	Reference(s)
Eating Disorders Inventory	Self-report	Standardized measure of psychological traits and symptom clusters presumed to have relevance to understanding and treatment of eating disorders, 11 subscales presented in 6-point, forced choice format; three scales assess attitudes and behaviors concerning eating, weight, and shape; eight more scales assess more general psychological traits; completion time: 20 minutes	Garner DM, Olmstead MJ, Polivy J: Development and validation of a multidimensional eating disorder inventory for anorexia nervosa and bulimia. Int J Eat Disorders Inventory 1983, 2:15-34. Garner DM: The Eating Disorders Inventory-2 Professional Manual. Odessa, Fla, Psychological Assessment Resources, 1991. Garner DM: The Eating Disorders Inventory-2 (EDI-2), in Outcomes Assessments in Clinical Practice. Edited by Sederer LI, Dickey B. Baltimore, Williams & Wilkins, 1996, pp 92-96
Eating Disorders Questionnaire	Self-report	Questions address eating disorders symptoms, associated symptoms, time course, treatment	Mitchell JE, Hatsukami D, Eckert E, Pyle RL: The Eating Disorders Questionnaire. Psychopharmacol Bull 1985, 21:1025-1043
Questionnaire of Eating and Weight Patterns	Self-report	Measures the nature and quantity of binge eating to assess binge-eating disorder	Yanovski SZ: Binge eating disorder: current knowledge and future directions. Obesity Res 1993, 1:306-320. Nangle DW, Johnson WG, Carr-Nangle RD, Engler LB: Binge eating disorder and the proposed DSM-IV criteria: psychometric analysis of the Questionnaire of Eating and Weight Patterns. Int J Eat Disord 1993, 16:147-157
Yale-Brown-Cornell Eating Disorder Scale	Clinical conducted interview	Includes a 65-item symptom checklist plus 19 questions, covering 18 general categories of rituals and preoccupations; requires 15 minutes or less to complete	Mazure CM, Halmi KA, Sunday SR, Romano SJ, Einhorn AN: Yale-Brown-Cornell Eating Disorder Scale: development, use, reliability and validity. J Psychiatr Res 1994, 28:425-445. Sunday SR, Halmi KA, Einhorn AN: The Yale-Brown-Cornell Eating Disorder Scale: a new scale to assess eating disorders symptomatology. Int J Eat Disord 1995, 18:237-245

Source: American Psychiatric Association. Reprinted with permission from the Diagnostic and Statistical Manual of Mental Disorders, Fourth Edition, Text Revision. Copyright 2000.

Brief Eating Disorders Screening Tool (SCOFF)

Score one point for every "yes" answer.
A score of ≥ 2 indicates a likely case of anorexia nervosa or bulimia.

1. Do you make yourself sick because you feel uncomfortably full?

2. Do you worry you have lost control over how much you eat?

3. Have you recently lost more than 14 pounds in a 3-month period?

4. Do you believe yourself to be fat when others say you are too thin?

5. Would you say that food dominates your life?

Source: Morgan JF et al. The SCOFF questionnaire: Assessment of a new screening tool for eating disorders. BMJ 319:1467-8; December 4, 1999.

Sample Questions to Assess Eating Attitudes and Behaviors

The following questions can help guide a brief assessment of eating behaviors.

1. Why do you want to lose weight? (Note any answers that suggest depression or isolation, such as "So I will have more friends.")
2. Do you feel like your eating is out of control? Do you ever feel scared that you will eat more than you want to?
3. Are you scared that if you stop dieting you will gain weight (again)?
4. Do you ever have trouble keeping your food down?
5. Are there any foods that you used to like to eat that you won't eat anymore? Why did you change? (Note any answer that suggests certain foods cause weight gain or health problems.)
6. Do you ever take a day off from exercise? What would happen if you couldn't exercise for a day? (Note any answers that suggest unreasonable fear of weight gain.)
7. How much of your day do you spend thinking about food and when and what you are going to eat? (Note any answer greater than 20%.)
8. Is the way you're eating affecting your work/school/social life/family?
9. Did you know there are specialists who help with these feelings/situations?

Assessment Questions for Restricting Behaviors

The following questions can help guide a thorough assessment of eating behaviors.

- What is your eating like throughout the day?
- Are you on a diet right now? What diets have you tried in the past?
- Are there any foods you prefer not to eat? What foods are you avoiding? Why? Do you miss any of those foods?
- Is there anything you used to like that you won't eat any more?
- Do you think you're getting enough to eat? Do you have any signs that you're not eating enough? Such as:
  - ➢ Recent weight loss?
  - ➢ Low energy during the day?
  - ➢ Difficulty sleeping?
  - ➢ Cold all the time?
  - ➢ Missing menstrual cycles?
  - ➢ Feeling faint or dizzy when you stand up?
  - ➢ Feeling chest pain or shortness of breath?
  - ➢ Thinking about food "all the time"?

Assessment Questions for Binge Eating Behaviors

The following questions can help guide a thorough assessment of eating behaviors.

- Do you ever worry that you'll get out of control around food? Or eat much more than you wanted to?
- Is it just a worry, or does it sometimes happen?
- What foods are your "weakness"? Do you try to avoid them? What happens when you are around them eventually?
- Can you give me an example of what you might eat that feels like it was way too much? Does this happen often? Or once in a while? Every day?
- Are you usually ravenous when you start to eat?
- Do you ever stop before you feel full?
- Do you always eat everything on your plate?
- What are meals like with your family?
- Is your eating different when you're alone?
- Do you visit the kitchen at non-meal times?
- Do you ever sleep walk to the kitchen at night? Or find empty packages in the morning that surprise you?

Assessment Questions for Purging Behaviors

Note: When assessing for potentially dangerous practices, it is wise to avoid making suggestions that a patient might implement. In other words, use general terms and do not indicate that any of these methods successfully promote weight loss.

- Do you ever feel guilty after you eat? What do you do in that situation?
- Do you ever feel like you need to get rid of the food you ate, or undo it? What do you do to make that feeling go away?
- Do you have any trouble keeping your food down?
- Does it come up automatically, or do you force it?
- How do you force it?
- How often do you struggle to keep your food down?
- Are there any foods that you feel comfortable keeping down? What are they?
- Is anyone else in your family dieting? Do you think anyone in your family has an eating disorder?
- How do family members react to your weight?

Assessment Questions for Compulsive Exercise, Body Dysmorphia and Other Obsessive Behaviors

The following questions relate to behaviors that are often associated with eating disorders.

- What kind of exercise do you like? How often do you participate?
- Do you ever plan rest days? Or do you ever realize you don't have time to exercise? How do you feel on those days you don't exercise?
- Is your eating different on days you exercise? Days you don't exercise?
- What other activities do you like? What does your family do together?
- How much of your day are you thinking about food, eating and your weight?
- How often do you weigh yourself? What are you checking for when you weigh through the day?
- How do you feel when you find out your weight? How does it affect your day?
- Do you eat differently depending on your weight? Do you eat differently before a medical weigh-in?
- Where do you keep your scale? How would it feel if your scale wasn't there?
- How would you like to change your body? Is there one specific part that you notice the most? How will you know when it's fixed? Do you check it?

Physical Signs of Eating Disorders

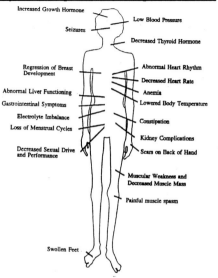

Increased Growth Hormone

Low Blood Pressure

Seizures

Decreased Thyroid Hormone

Regression of Breast Development

Abnormal Heart Rhythm

Decreased Heart Rate

Abnormal Liver Functioning

Anemia

Gastrointestinal Symptoms

Lowered Body Temperature

Electrolyte Imbalance

Loss of Menstrual Cycles

Constipation

Kidney Complications

Decreased Sexual Drive and Performance

Scars on Back of Hand

Muscular Weakness and Decreased Muscle Mass

Painful muscle spasm

Swollen Feet

Source: Anderson. Practical Comprehensive Treatment of Anorexia Nervosa and Bulimia. Pp 45, 51. Used with permission. Copyright 1987 John Hopkins University Press.

Physical Complications of Anorexia Nervosa

Organ System	Symptoms	Signs	Laboratory Test Results
Whole body	Weakness, lassitude	Malnutrition	Low weight/body mass index, low body fat percentage
Central nervous system	Apathy, poor concentration	Cognitive impairment; depressed, irritable mood	CT:ventricular enlargement; MRI: decreased gray and white matter
Cardiovascular and peripheral vascular	Palpitations, weakness, dizziness, shortness of breath, chest pain, cold extremities	Irregular, weak, slow pulse; marked orthostatic blood pressure changes; peripheral vasoconstriction with acrocyanosis	ECG: bradycardia, arrhythmias; Q-T prolongation (dangerous sign)
Skeletal	Bone pain with exercise	Point tenderness; short stature/arrested skeletal growth	X-rays or DEXA bone scan for pathological stress fractures; bone densitometry for bone mineral density assessment for osteopenia
Muscular	Weakness, muscle aches	Muscle wasting	Muscle enzyme abnormalities in severe malnutrition
Reproductive	Arrested psychosexual maturation or interest; loss of libido	Loss of menses or primary amenorrhea; arrested sexual development or regression of secondary sex characteristics; fertility problems; higher rates of pregnancy complications	Hypoestrogenemia; prepubertal patterns of LH, FSH secretion; lack of follicular development/ dominant follicle on pelvic ultrasound

(continued)

Physical Complications of Anorexia Nervosa

(continued)

Organ System	Symptoms	Signs	Laboratory Test Results
Endocrine, metabolic	Fatigue; cold intolerance; diuresis; vomiting	Low body temperature (hypothermia)	Elevated serum cortisol; increase in rT3 ("reverse" T3); dehydration; electrolyte abnormalities; hypophosphatemia (especially on refeeding); hypoglycemia (rare)
Hematologic	Fatigue; cold intolerance	Rare bruising/clotting abnormalities	Anemia; neutropenia with relative lymphocytosis; thrombocytopenia; low erythrocyte sedimentation rate; rarely clotting factor abnormalities
Gastrointestinal	Vomiting; abdominal pain; bloating; obstipation; constipation	Abdominal distension with meals; abnormal bowel sounds	Delayed gastric emptying; occasionally abnormal liver function test results
Genitourinary		Pitting edema	Elevated BUN; low glomerular filtration rate; greater formation of renal calculi; hypovolemic nephropathy
Integument	Change in hair	Lanugo	

Source: American Psychiatric Association. Reprinted with permission from the Diagnostic and Statistical Manual of Mental Disorders, Fourth Edition, Text Revision, Copyright 2000.

Physical Complications of Bulimia Nervosa

Organ System	Symptoms	Signs	Laboratory Test Results
Metabolic	Weakness; irritability	Poor skin turgor	Dehydration (urine specific gravity; osmolality); serum electrolytes: hypokalemic, hypochloremic alkalosis in those who vomit; hypomagnesemia and hypophosphatemia in laxative abusers
Gastrointestinal	Abdominal pain and discomfort in vomiters; occasionally automatic vomiting; obstipation; constipation; bowel irregularities and bloating in laxative abusers	Occasionally blood-streaked vomitus; vomiters may occasionally have gastritis, esophagitis, gastroesophageal erosions, esophageal dysmotility patterns (including gastroesophageal reflux, and, very rarely, Mallory-Weiss [esophageal] or gastric tears); may have increased rates of pancreatitis; chronic laxative abusers may show colonic dysmotility or melanosis coli	
Reproductive	Fertility problems	Spotty/scanty menstrual periods	May be hypoestrogenemic

(continued)

Physical Complications of Bulimia Nervosa

(continued)

Organ System	Symptoms	Signs	Laboratory Test Results
Oropharyngeal	Dental decay; pain in pharynx; swollen cheeks and neck (painless)	Dental caries with erosion of dental enamel, particularly lingual surface of incisors; erythema of pharynx; enlarged salivary glands	X-rays confirm erosion of dental enamel; elevated serum amylase associated with benign parotid hyperplasia
Integument		Scarring on dorsum of hand (Russell's sign)	
Cardiomuscular (in ipecac abusers)	Weakness; palpitation	Cardiac abnormalities; muscle weakness	Cardiomyopathy and peripheral myopathy

Source: American Psychiatric Association. Reprinted with permission from the Diagnostic and Statistical Manual of Mental Disorders, Fourth Edition, Text Revision, Copyright 2000.

Recommended Laboratory Assessments for Eating Disorders

Basic analyses	Patient Indication
Blood chemistry studies	Consider for all patients with eating disorders
Serum electrolyte level	*especially when purging is suspected
Blood urea nitrogen (BUN) level	
Creatinine level	
Thyroid function test	*especially in unexplained weight loss or weight gain
Complete blood count (CBC)	
Urinalysis	* include tox screen and pregnancy test when appropriate
Additional analyses - Consider for malnourished and severely symptomatic patients	
Calcium level	
Magnesium level	
Phosphorus level	
Liver function tests	
Electrocardiogram (EKG), Stress Test, Stress ECHO	*especially in rapid weight loss or with reports of chest pain or syncope

Source: American Psychiatric Association. Reprinted with permission from the Diagnostic and Statistical Manual of Mental Disorders, Fourth Edition, Text Revision, Copyright 2000.

Symptoms of Eating Disorders that May Require Urgent Care

- Dizziness, fainting, shortness of breath
- Chest pain
- Blood in stool or vomit
- Prolonged/painful constipation or diarrhea
- Uncontrollable inability to keep down any food or fluids

Symptoms that May Require Further Medical Assessment

- Indications of gastrointestinal damage:
  - After or during eating, food comes up automatically.
  - Persistent heartburn, constipation, bloating, gas, "stomachache" and/or nausea.
  - Fullness after few bites (early satiety) and long after meals (delayed gastric emptying).
- Indications of iron-deficiency anemia:
  - Fatigue and low energy.
  - Persistent and/or chronic headaches.
  - Craving ice

(continued)

Symptoms that May Require Further Medical Assessment

(continued)

- Indications of cardiovascular damage:
  - Rapid weight loss (causes muscle loss, often damaging the heart muscle).
  - Chest pain when exercising or at rest.
  - Pounding heartbeats or skipping beats.
  - Use of ipecac syrup as an emetic (ipecac is a vomiting aid that can damage the heart).
- Indications of skeletal damage:
  - Long-term poor nutrition, especially low calcium intake, low protein intake, and/or excessive caffeine intake.
  - Amenorrhea (adequate estrogen is required to build bone); either 3 missed menstrual cycles or over age 16 without menarche. Periods induced with oral hormones have not been shown to protect bone mass.
  - Unexpected short stature indicative of stunting.
  - History of bone fractures from minimal contact, multiple fractures, or stress fractures.
  - History of excessive exercise leading to weight loss.

(continued)

Symptoms that May Require Further Medical Assessment

(continued)

- Indications of endocrine abnormality:
  - Difficulty becoming or staying pregnant.
  - Amenorrhea (either 3 missed menstrual cycles or over age 16 without menarche) or oligomenorrhea (irregular cycles).
  - Fatigue (may be related to thyroid levels).
  - Unexplained or dramatic weight change (loss or gain), especially at a young age or surrounding menarche or menopause.
  - Difficulty losing weight even though caloric intake is low.
  - Symptoms of hypoglycemia (irritability, loss of clarity, shaking, sweating, weakness, dizziness several hours after eating) that do not resolve with normal eating.
  - Symptoms of diabetes/hyperglycemia (extreme thirst, extreme hunger, excessive urination, waking in the night to urinate).
  - Early puberty.
  - Skin tags, severe acne, brown patches of skin, excessive facial hair in women.

Psychiatric Disorders that May Occur with Eating Disorders

- Attention deficit disorder (assess all patients with high caffeine intake)
- Bipolar disorder (more common with bulimia)
- Body dysmorphic disorder (obsession over one specific body part)
- Chemical dependency (including prescription drugs, alcohol, street drugs)
- Depression, anxiety disorder (common with all eating disorder types)
- Obsessive/compulsive disorder (in other areas besides food and eating)
- Post-traumatic stress disorder (especially including self-harm)

Any combination of these can occur together. Poor nutrition caused by an eating disorder can exacerbate symptoms of other psychiatric disorders. Treatment must focus on appropriate care of all diagnoses and contributing factors. Often patients struggling to overcome chemical dependency will realize for the first time that they have an eating disorder as well. Eating disorder onset may also coincide with attempts to recover from a chemical dependency. More research is needed to identify factors that eating disorders have in common with other psychiatric disorders and how these disorders influence eating disorder risk and development.

Role of Psychiatric Medications in Eating Disorders

- Eating disorders and self-harm are self-medicating – they cause brain chemistry changes similar to medications.

- Medications can provide relief so that patients can change behaviors without being "hooked" on them; similar to a nicotine patch. Medication does not automatically stop all behaviors but can provide symptom management, stop ruminations, and help provide clearer thinking.

- Side effects, non-compliance, and running out of medication should be reported to the prescribing physician immediately. Patients should be discouraged from self-diagnosing, increasing or decreasing their medication without the guidance of their psychiatrist. Psychoactive medications have differing half-lives, and some can be dangerous if stopped without weaning.

- Medications may be needed only temporarily for some patients, while other patients may need medication continually to maintain quality of life.

Psychiatric Medications and Eating-Related Effects

Brand Name	Generic Name	Appetite & Weight	Comments/Other Effects
Adderall	amphetamine salts	both down	Can cause dramatic weight loss and/or difficulty gaining weight; encourage eating before meds
Ambien	zolpidem		Can cause binge eating/night eating with amnesia; should be taken only when patient is ready for bed
Ativan	lorazepam		
Celexa	citalopram	both up	
Clozaril	clozapine	wt up (dramatic)	May cause extreme weight gain May cause severe constipation
Cogentin	benztropine		
Cylert	pemoline	both down	Monitor growth in children
Cymbalta	duloxetine	either way	
Dalmane	flurazepam	either way	
Depakene Depakote	valproic acid	both up	May increase cholesterol May cause false positive ketones
Desyrel	trazodone	either way	Possible anemia, edema
Dexedrine	dextro-amphetamine	both down	May be abused for weight loss; Ca or Mg supplements may increase & Vit C may decrease drug efficacy

(continued)

Psychiatric Medications and Eating-Related Effects

Brand Name	Generic Name	Appetite & Weight	Comments/Other Effects
Dilantin	phenytoin		May decrease levels of folate, cholesterol, Ca, Vit D; >5mg/wk folate lowers drug availability May increase blood glucose
Effexor	venlafaxine	either way	
Elavil Pamelor	amitriptyline nortriptyline	both up, may crave carbs and sweets	May elevate blood glucose; increases riboflavin needs; high fiber diet may decrease efficacy
Eskalith Lithotabs Lithonate Lithane	lithium	wt and thirst up but may decrease app	Drink 2-3 L non-caloric fluids daily and keep sodium intake consistent; Limit xanthine (coffee, tea, cola) May increase serum electrolytes May cause bloating
Klonopin	clonazepam	app down, thirst up, wt either way	
Lexapro	escitalopram	both up	
Luvox	fluvoxamine	either way	May increase cholesterol

(continued)

Psychiatric Medications and Eating-Related Effects
(continued)

Brand Name	Generic Name	Appetite & Weight	Comments/Other Effects
Mellaril	thioridazine	both up	May increase cholesterol, glucose Increases riboflavin needs
Nardil	phenelzine	both up	MAOI – monitor tyramine intake
Navane	thiothixene	both up	Increases riboflavin needs
Norpramin Tofranil	desipramine imipramine	both up, may crave sweets	High fiber may decrease efficacy Increases riboflavin needs May elevate blood glucose
Paxil	paroxetine	both up	Weight gain can be dramatic
Prozac	fluoxetine	app down, wt up or dn	FDA approved to treat bulimia May lower Na
Restoril	temazepam		
Risperdal	respiridone	both up	May lower Na, Hgb, Hct
Ritalin	methylphenidate	both down	Can cause dramatic weight loss and/or difficulty gaining weight; encourage eating before meds
Seraquel	quetiapine	wt up	

(continued)

Psychiatric Medications and Eating-Related Effects

(continued)

Brand Name	Generic Name	Appetite & Weight	Comments/Other Effects
Sinequan	doxepin	both up, thirst up, may crave sweets	High fiber may decrease efficacy. May elevate blood glucose
Tegretol	carbamazepine	app down	
Thorazine	chlorpromazine	Both up	May increase cholesterol, blood glucose; Increases riboflavin needs
Topamax	topiramate	Both down	Decreases binge-eating; not FDA approved for this indication. Can increase lactic acid and cause acidosis/kidney stones
Valium	diazepam	variable	May cause constipation
Wellbutrin	bupropion	Both down	Contraindicated with anorexia or bulimia due to potential seizures
Xanax	alprazolam	unpredict-able effects on appetite and wt	

(continued)

Psychiatric Medications and Eating-Related Effects
(continued)

Brand Name	Generic Name	Appetite & Weight	Comments/Other Effects
Zoloft	sertraline	either way	
Zyprexa	olanzapine	Both up (dramatic)	Can cause diabetes, ketosis May increase cholesterol and/or triglycerides

Psychoactive medication efficacy varies on an individual patient basis. Significant weight change (e.g. weight gain or weight loss in excess of 10% of body weight) may necessitate modification in dosage. Refer patients who have gained or lost weight to their prescribing physician for reassessment.

Refer patients reporting abuse or excessive use of non-prescribed medications or over-the-counter medications (including diet pills, caffeine-containing beverages or pills, ephedrine, anabolic steroids, cough medicine, emetics, anti-emetics and so on) to a psychiatrist for evaluation. Often patients self-medicate when they have legitimate medication needs that have not been recognized.

Compiled with information from Barry Knezek, MD, and Physician's Desk Reference.

Ultimate Treatment Goals for All Eating Disorders

- Medical/physical stability and physical health restoration.
- "Normalized" (non-restrictive) eating, including variety, balance, nutritional adequacy and comfort with food.
- "Normalized" (not excessive) and safe physical activities.
- Absence of purging behaviors.
- Healthy coping mechanisms for triggers.
- Improved mental health.
- Supportive social structure in place to prevent relapse during stress.

There is no known vaccination or permanent cure for eating disorders, only long-term management. Whether complete recovery is possible is still debated, but many patients have complete resolution of symptoms. Under stressful life circumstances, symptoms may flare up at any time in the future.

Initial Meal Planning Guidelines for All Eating Disorder Types

- Plan 4 to 6 eating opportunities per day.
- Meals and snacks can be the same size, if desired.
- Work within a patient's preferred schedule, as long as it provides adequate eating opportunities.
- Allow no more than 4 hours between eating opportunities in order to prevent hypoglycemia, extreme hunger, poor judgment, and/or the temptation to binge.
- Encourage small portion sizes to provide a comfortable volume; as much as possible avoid eating anything that causes the desire to purge.
- Recommend including a source of protein and a source of carbohydrate at every meal and snack.
- If fluids have been used to reduce caloric intake, or induce purging, avoid beverages at meals.
- Work within patient preferences. Do not include foods known to be triggers for bingeing, purging, self-harm, or extreme regret. Incorporate new foods slowly.
- Encourage decreased reliance on caffeine and calorie-free foods and drinks.
- Encourage patient and family to accept this meal plan, even though it is not the "normal" eating they are ultimately hoping to achieve.

(continued)

Initial Meal Planning Guidelines for All Eating Disorder Types
(continued)

- Remind concerned patients and family members that it is acceptable to become "obsessed" with the meal plan for the time being. This is an improvement from being captive to disordered eating or obsessed with starvation. In time the meal plan will not be necessary, as the patient internalizes normal eating patterns. For now it is essential to minimize the damage of malnutrition.
- Use any meal plan model that works, for example:
  - ➤ Exchange plan – using the Diabetic Exchange lists for meal planning
  - ➤ Prepared meals – from the hospital kitchen or an outside delivery service
  - ➤ Calorie counting – teaching calorie counting may not or may not be necessary, but if a patient is already familiar with calories in food, train him or her to use this knowledge to meet an appropriate daily caloric goal
  - ➤ Liquid nutritional supplements – can be used to supplement food intake or as total nutrition if needed, via tubefeeding or orally
  - ➤ Menu plan, with or without options – Specify exactly what and how much a patient should attempt to eat at specific times of day. Two to four possible options may be provided depending on patient's comfort with making decisions. If patient is uncomfortable with choices, devise specific menus for each day of the week.

__Additional Meal Planning Guidelines for Anorexia Nervosa__

- Estimate current caloric intake and set daily goals 200-300 calories higher.
- Divide recommended calories evenly between 6 eating opportunities per day, or offer 3 larger meals and 3 smaller snacks. Discourage meal skipping and "catching up" later or "saving" calories for a later meal.
- Solid food may not provide adequate caloric intake, making liquid supplementation essential.
- Use weight changes as a guide to increasing daily calorie goals. Increases can be more rapid in a highly monitored setting, or may be very slow as needed.
- Provide supervision and support for patient during and after meal times until a pattern of normal eating and comfort with eating is established.
- Mealtime conversations should avoid topics related to food, weight, eating, etc.
- "Diet," low-calorie, reduced fat, low-carbohydrate, calorie-free, and nutrient poor foods, drinks, and condiments should be included in meals only after consultation between patient and dietitian as to their appropriate use.
- Identify ritualistic food behaviors, such as reheating food repeatedly during a meal, exercising during a meal, abnormal mixtures of food, and excessive cutting or chewing of food. Discuss these rituals with patient at a non-meal time to determine their purpose and encourage their discontinuation.

Additional Meal Planning Guidelines for Binge Eating and Bulimia

- Binge eating patients, whether they purge or not, often feel that restricting is essential to weight loss, resulting in more bingeing. Encourage patients to eat regularly to prevent the urge to overeat or eat rapidly.
- Eating less than 6 times a day may be adequate if portions can be small enough for comfort.
- Note that eating at all can cause extreme guilt and/or purging, even if the amount consumed is considered very small or "normal."
- Eating under stress is more likely to result in bingeing and/or purging.
- Encourage a calm environment before preparing, serving, or eating food. If patient is overwhelmed, request that they take a break before eating to calm down. A structured meal plan can provide support during meal preparation. Encourage patient to delegate child feeding and meal clean up to others.
- Provide support to patient during after meals and encourage expression of feelings or distracting activities. Encourage patient to stay out of the bathroom for up to an hour after eating.
- Initial meal plan should not include any foods that patient is unwilling or unable to keep down.
- Carbonated beverages may promote indigestion or vomiting, and should be limited after consultation with the dietitian regarding appropriate use.

Additional Meal Strategies for All Eating Disorder Types

- Discourage checking weight after meals.
- Supervise patient during and after meals for support and guidance. Provide distracting activities after meals and/or activities that promote acceptance and/or expression of the feelings that surface after eating.
- Encourage patient to eat with others. Provide healthy role models to eat with patients if possible. Observing healthy eaters eating is therapeutic even if they are strangers.
- If patient complains of unusual thirst, excessive hunger, or lack of appetite, consider the appetite-related effects of prescribed medications.
- Consider symptom management for nausea, indigestion, diarrhea, constipation, and flatulence that may be the natural effects of malnutrition. These may not be necessary long term, but may promote nutrition in the short term.
- Limit caffeinated beverages as they impair appetite and hunger. If patient is dependent on caffeine, consider offering caffeine pills to taper intake without associated withdrawal symptoms.

Social Eating Strategies for All Eating Disorder Types

- Eat a little snack an hour or so before you go out to eat. Being too hungry when you order makes it hard to choose appropriately.

- Don`t fill up on chips or bread unless they are what you really want for dinner.

- Pay attention to how full you feel and stop when you are satisfied. Don`t let anyone take your plate until you`re ready.

- Alcohol alters your judgment about what and how much to eat. Consider leaving it out of your meals until you are in a routine.

- Decide in advance if you want to have dessert. Check the dessert menu, see if there is something you would like, and order the rest of your meal accordingly. Dessert is part of your meal, not something to add on after you `re full. Consider a milkshake as a dessert, not a beverage, unless you need the added calories.

- In a restaurant where portion sizes are overwhelming, share an entrée with someone, order an appetizer for a meal, ask for a child`s portion, or take home leftovers.

- Order water with your meal unless you need to increase your caloric intake. Soft drinks provide calories with no nutrients yet don`t satisfy your hunger, your thirst, or your need for food.

- Eat slowly and focus on the conversation and ambiance – enjoy eating out!

- If you are not comfortable eating out, but would like to attend a social function, eat in advance, order water with lime or lemon to sip on, and tell anyone who comments on your non-eating, "No, thank you, I already ate; I just came to enjoy the event."

Protecting Patients from the Harmful Effects of Purging

- Restrict patient's access to laxatives, emetics, and diet pills.
- Educate patient regarding the harmful effects of purging on digestive system and overall health. Do not expect scare tactics to work, but patient should at least be introduced to the workings of the digestive system and the risks and minimal effects of their chosen method(s).
- Although purging often does not "work" as a weight loss tool, patients feel "lighter" and "emptier" after purging. Educate that this does not necessarily mean they have lost weight, i.e. body mass.
- Encourage patient to drink water or an electrolyte-replacement beverage mixed with water after purging to replenish fluids and electrolytes.
- Discourage patient from brushing teeth immediately after vomiting, as this can further erode and damage tooth enamel. Rinsing with water or baking soda and water is considered less damaging.
- If a patient cannot keep down any food or fluids, and/or is unable to decrease the frequency of purging behaviors, consider a higher level of care where patient can be more closely monitored and supported.

Details of Restrictive Eating Styles

Type	Avoids	Eats	Philosophy
Semi-Vegetarian	Beef, Pork	Poultry, Eggs, Seafood, Dairy	Varies by individual. Motivation may be health-related, animal rights based, or linked to a past bad experience. "Live 'in balance with nature" for a healthy mind, body and spirit. Eat as few calories as possible of nutrient-dense foods in an effort to prolong lifespan.
Pesco-Vegetarian	Beef, Pork, Poultry	Seafood, Dairy, Eggs	
Lacto-Ovo Vegetarian	Beef, Pork, Poultry, Seafood	Dairy, Eggs	
Lacto-Vegetarian	Beef, Pork, Poultry, Seafood, Eggs	Dairy	
Vegan	All animal products	All plant foods	
Macrobiotic	All animal products, Coffee, Processed foods, certain fruits and juice, Artificial ingredients	Beans, Vegetables, Tofu, Whole Grains, Tea	
Calorie Restricting	Processed sugars, Flour, "Calorie-sparse" foods, Red meat, White rice	Vegetables, Small amounts of fish	

THE VEGETARIAN FOOD PYRAMID

A DAILY GUIDE TO FOOD CHOICES

LOW-FAT OR NON-FAT
MILK, YOGURT, CHEESE
AND FORTIFIED
ALTERNATIVE GROUP
2-3 SERVINGS
EAT MODERATELY

WHOLE GRAIN
BREAD, CEREAL,
PASTA, AND RICE
GROUP
6-11 SERVINGS
EAT LIBERALLY

VEGETABLE GROUP
3-5 SERVINGS
EAT GENEROUSLY

VEGETABLE FATS AND OILS,
SWEETS, AND SALT
EAT SPARINGLY

LEGUME, NUT, SEED AND
MEAT ALTERNATIVE GROUP
2-3 SERVINGS
EAT MODERATELY

FRUIT GROUP
2-4 SERVINGS
EAT GENEROUSLY

Vegetarian Food Pyramid

Types of Binge Eating

Binge eating can be simply a natural consequence of restrictive eating/starvation. Individuals who have been calorie deprived for any reason may feel compelled to eat quickly, eat until they are uncomfortably full, and/or eat larger portions than normal.

Binge eating can also be related to emotional needs, and/or a combination of all of the above. Hunger-related binge eating must be resolved first with adequate and timely nourishment. Then the emotion-related binge eating will be more recognizable, treatment can change focus from nutrition education to nutrition problem-solving, and psychotherapy can address the underlying issues.

- Deprivation-sensitive - caused by actual or mental restriction of certain foods or food in general. "I'll diet tomorrow, so I'll eat a lot now."

- Affect-triggered - eating in response to strong emotions. "I'm so angry at my husband, I'm going to finish his last piece of pie."

- Addictive or Dissociative - eating used to "numb out," avoid, or procrastinate. "I'm bored. Eating would fill the time."

Source: France White, MS, RD www.innerescapes.com

Food Exchanges for Meal Planning

Source: Printed with permission by Andrea Chernus, MS, RD www.nutritionhandouts.com

STARCH
EACH SERVING CONTAINS
80 CALORIES
15 GRAMS CARBOHYDRATE

CEREALS / GRAINS
Cold unsweetened cereal: ¾ cup
Flour (dry): 3 Tbsp
Hot cereal: ½ cup cooked
Pasta: ⅓ cup cooked
Rice (white or brown): ⅓ cup cooked
Wheat germ: 3 Tbsp

BREAD
Bagel: 1 oz. (½ small; ¼ large)
Bread: 1 slice (1 oz.)
Breadsticks: 2 (4" x ½")
English muffin: ½
Hamburger or hot dog roll: ½ (1 oz.)
Roll: small, plain 1 oz.
Tortilla: 1 6" diameter
Waffle: 4-1/2" square, reduced fat

STARCHY VEGETABLES
Baked beans: ⅓ cup
Corn, cooked: ½ cup
Mixed vegetables (corn, peas): ½ cup
Peas, green: ½ cup
Plantain: ½ cup
Potato, white: small, 3 oz.
Potato mashed: ½ cup
Squash, winter: 1 cup cooked
Yam / Sweet potato: ½ cup

MILK
ONE SERVING CONTAINS
90-150 CALORIES
12 GRAMS CARBOHYDRATE
Cottage cheese: ½ cup
1 cup milk or yogurt
(non-fat or 1% preferred)

CRACKERS / SNACKS
Animal crackers: 8
Graham crackers: 3 2-1/2" squares
Melba toast: 4 slices
Popcorn: 3 cups popped, no fat added
Pretzels: 3 oz.
Saltine crackers: 6

FRUIT
ONE SERVING CONTAINS
60 CALORIES
15 GRAM CARBOHYDRATE
Apple, raw (2" across)
Applesauce (no sugar added): ½ cup
Banana (9" long 4 oz)
Cantaloupe: 1 cup
Cherries: 12
Canned fruit: ½ cup
Grapes: 17 small
Orange: 1 medium
Peach: 1 medium
Pear: 1 large
Pineapple: ¾ cup fresh
Raisins: 2 Tbsp
Strawberries: 1-¼ cup whole berries
Juice: orange, grapefruit: ½ cup
cranberry, grape, prune: ⅓ cup

BEANS / PEAS / LENTILS
(1 starch and 1 lean meat):
Beans & Peas: garbanzo, kidney, white,
pinto, split peas: ½ cup
Lima beans: ½ cup
Lentil: ½ cup

MEATS
LEAN (55 CALORIES/SVG)
Cottage cheese: ¼ cup
Egg whites: 2
Fresh & frozen fish: 1 oz.
Fat free cheese: 1 oz.
Lamb (chop, roast): 1 oz.
Lean beef (sirloin, round or flank): 1 oz.
Skinless white poultry: 1 oz.
Tuna canned in water: 1 oz.
Any processed meats with
1 gram of fat or less: 1 oz.

MEDIUM / HIGH FAT (76-100 CALORIES / SVG)
Beef (rib, chuck, rump) 1 oz.
Cheese: 1 oz.
Tuna canned in oil: 1 oz.
Pork (spareribs, ground, and
pork sausage): 1 oz.
Eggs: 1
Peanut butter: 1 T
Soy milk: 1 cup
Tofu: 4 oz. or ½ cup

VEGETABLES
ONE SERVING CONTAINS
25 CALORIES
5 GRAMS CARBOHYDRATE
One serving is ½ cup cooked
or one cup raw:

Asparagus	Mushrooms
Beets	Okra
Broccoli	Peppers
Brussels sprouts	Pea pods
Cabbage	Spinach
Carrots	Tomatoes
Celery	Wax Beans
Green Beans	Zucchini
Greens	

FATS
EACH SERVING CONTAINS
45 CALORIES
Avocado: 1/8 medium
Bacon: 1 slice
Butter: 1 tsp
Margarine: 1 tsp
Reduced fat margarine: 1 Tbsp
Mayonnaise: 1 tsp
Reduced fat mayonnaise: 1 T
Nuts/Seeds: 1 T (about 6 nuts)
Oil: 1 tsp
Salad dressing: 1 T
Reduced fat salad dressing: 2T

FREE FOODS
EACH SERVING HAS LESS
THAN 20 CALORIES
Bullion, diet sodas, coffee,
tea, sugar free gum & mints,
herbs, lemon juice, mustard
sugar substitutes, garlic, fresh
Worcestershire sauce,
1-1/2 large pickles, 1 T each;
catsup or taco sauce

Common Serving Size Equivalents

1	3 ounces of meat is about the size and thickness of a deck of playing cards or an audiotape cassette.	= (deck of cards)
2	A medium apple or peach is about the size of a tennis ball.	= (tennis ball)
3	1 oz of cheese is about the size of 4 stacked dice.	= (dominoes/dice)
4	1/2 cup of ice cream is about the size of a racquetball or tennis ball.	= (ball)
5	1 cup of mashed potatoes or broccoli is about the size of your fist.	= (fist)
6	1 teaspoon of butter or peanut butter is about the size of the tip of your thumb.	= (thumb)
7	1 ounce of nuts or small candies equals one handful.	= 1 OZ.

Most Important
Especially if you're cutting calories, remember to keep your diet nutritious.

2-4 servings from the Milk Group for calcium
2-3 servings from the Meat Group for iron
3-5 servings from the Vegetable Group for vitamin A
2-4 servings from the Fruit Group for vitamin C
6-11 servings from the Grain Group for fiber

Source: Wheat Foods Council. Reprinted with permission.

Nutrition Support Indications in Eating Disorders

Nutrition Support (enteral feeding, tube feeding) may be required in the following situations:

- Patient refuses any oral caloric intake.
- Patient is medically unstable/in danger due to low weight and/or low intake.
- Continuing rapid weight loss despite improved intake.
- Weight or intake has not improved to necessary level or has fallen below what was agreed upon by patient and physician.
- Malnutrition is causing inability to think clearly/proceed in treatment.
- Although patient is willing, gastrointestinal dysfunction is restricting intake.
- Excessive energy needs (patient is hypermetabolic and unable to meet caloric needs orally). Additional calories may be supplemented in a nighttime tube feeding.

Notes: Nutrition support is not a punishment and should not be referred to as such. Family members may have strong feelings and/or misconceptions regarding nutrition support and if so, will need education and guidance in response to their concerns.

Adapted from SCAN'S PULSE, Spring 1999, Vol.17, No. 2, official publication of Sports, Cardiovascular, and Wellness Nutritionists (SCAN), American Dietetic Association, Chicago, IL.

Nutrition Support Options and Guidelines for Eating Disorders

- If patient is able to eat by mouth, provide the options of eating solid food, drinking liquid supplements, or nutrition support. A tube feeding can then be provided only when needed to provide supplementary nutrition, while encouraging appropriate eating behaviors at meal times.

- Options:
    - ➤ Bolus feed appropriate supplemental calories only at meal times
    - ➤ Bolus feed only uneaten calories to meet meal time goal
    - ➤ Nighttime continuous feed of uneaten or excessive calories

- TPN (Total Parenteral Nutrition, Intravenous Feeding) is only indicated in cases of digestive inability, such as pancreatitis, because it leads to loss of hunger cues and does not encourage the healthy eating behaviors necessary to recovery. TPN should be used when necessary, and for the shortest possible duration.

- When tube feeding is initiated in severely malnourished patients, it is possible to trigger refeeding syndrome, a life-threatening imbalance of electrolytes. Slow increases in volume are the best defense against complications.

(continued)

Possible Complications of Enteral Feeding in Eating Disorders

- Hypophosphatemia

- Hypokalemia

- Hypomagnesemia

- Vitamin deficiency
  (especially Thiamine)

- Hyponatremia

- Impaired glucose
  metabolism

- Fluid intolerance

- Diarrhea

- Constipation

- Gas and abdominal
  discomfort

- Clogged feeding tube

Note: Complications may result from client manipulation of feeding. Monitor tube feeding administration if possible before adjusting feeding regime. See next page for guidelines to minimize the risk of complications including refeeding syndrome.

Reprinted with permission, from SCAN'S PULSE, Winter 2000, Vol.18, No. 1, official publication of Sports, Cardiovascular, and Wellness Nutritionists (SCAN), American Dietetic Association, Chicago, IL.

Enteral Feeding Initiation Guidelines for Eating Disorders

- Ideally, enteral feeding is an adjunct, not the primary source of nutrition. Tube feeding is necessary only until adequate nutrients can be consumed by mouth.

- Protein repletion should begin at 1.2 to 1.5 g protein per kg ideal body weight in order to protect lean body tissue despite a hypocaloric diet.

- Calories should be in accordance with intake during starvation and the infusion should not exceed 25 to 50 cc/hr from the tube. Rapid progression increases the likelihood of complications.

- An isotonic, fiber-containing, polymeric formula is usually sufficient for nutritional repletion, unless impaired digestion or absorption indicates use of an elemental diet or peptide-based product.

- Fluid intolerance is exacerbated by excess carbohydrate introduction. Monitor carbohydrates in the meal plan and the feeding formula until weight gain is proven to be gradual and appropriate.

- Fluid requirements for the low-weight individual should be estimated at approximately 20 to 21 mL water per kg or 1 mL water per kcal formula.

- Gradually increase the feedings by 10 to 25 cc/h every 8 to 24 hours if tolerated until the target rate is achieved. Weaning can begin as soon as the tube feeding objectives are being met.

Reprinted with permission, from SCAN'S PULSE, Spring 1999, Vol.17, No. 2, official publication of Sports, Cardiovascular, and Wellness Nutritionists (SCAN), American Dietetic Association, Chicago, IL.

Minimizing the Risks of Refeeding Syndrome in Eating Disorders

Although cases of refeeding syndrome are rare, malnourished patients with advanced eating disorders are at particular risk because of the body's adaptation to malnourishment. This potential for danger is compounded if feeding is pursued aggressively.

1. Use isotonic enteral feedings and avoid high glucose formulas.

2. At initiation, limit carbohydrate calories to 150 – 200 g/day.

3. Maximize fat calories.

4. Initiate protein intake at 1.2 to 1.5 g/kg, as tolerated.

5. Maintain client on a hypocaloric diet through the first 3 to 5 days. Then gradually adjust calories upward toward full needs as tolerated. This may mean daily adjustments as minimal as 0 to 150 kcals per day until you are certain tolerance is consistent.

(continued)

Reprinted with permission, from SCAN'S PULSE, Winter 2000, Vol.18, No. 1, official publication of Sports, Cardiovascular, and Wellness Nutritionists (SCAN), American Dietetic Association, Chicago, IL.

Minimizing the Risks of Refeeding Syndrome in Eating Disorders
(continued)

   Close monitoring is critical, particularly during the first 5 to 7 days of enteral feeding. Lab values will often be normal or near normal in a malnourished state because of a variety of mechanisms, including dehydration (concentrates blood values of certain parameters), a slowed metabolic rate, and other adaptations to starvation, which mask the true medical frailty of the client. When nutrient repletion begins, lab values may change suddenly, creating potentially dangerous consequences.

- **Evaluate daily:** body weight, blood glucose, fluid input and output

- **Evaluate at least 3 times a week:** serum electrolytes, BUN and creatinine

- **Evaluate weekly:** albumin, pre-albumin, calcium and magnesium, serum electrolytes (phosphorus, potassium, sodium, magnesium), blood urea nitrogen (BUN), and creatinine until stable.

Reprinted with permission, from SCAN'S PULSE, Winter 2000, Vol.18, No. 1, official publication of Sports, Cardiovascular, and Wellness Nutritionists (SCAN), American Dietetic Association, Chicago, IL.

Additional Nutrition Support Guidelines for Bulimia

- Continuous drip tube feeding can give a damaged gastrointestinal system a chance to recuperate.

- A continuous drip is often preferable over bolus feedings, which are more likely to cause dumping syndrome, involuntary vomiting, and can be more easily purged.

- Monitor patients to help prevent purging or disconnection of tube or pump.

- Some patients can go from tube feeding to oral feeding without incident. Other patients will benefit from a post-surgical feeding progression as follows:

  - ➢ Clear liquids
  - ➢ Full liquids
  - ➢ Bland diet
  - ➢ Soft diet
  - ➢ Low fat diet
  - ➢ Regular diet (calorie controlled)

Oral/Enteral Nutrition Supplement Brand Equivalents

ROSS	NOVARTIS	NESTLE
Ensure® Osmolite®	Boost® Resource® Isocal® Isosource®	NuBasics® Nutren® 1.0
Ensure Plus®	Boost Plus® Resource Plus®	NuBasics® Plus
Ensure® Fiber with FOS	Boost® with Fiber	Nutren® Fiber
Ensure Plus® HN	Boost Plus® Resource Plus®	NuBasics® Plus
Ensure® High Protein	Boost® High Protein	NutriHeal™
Twocal® HN	Resource® 2.0 Deliver® 2.0	Nutren® 2.0
Jevity® 1 Cal	Fibersource™ Compleat® Ultracal®	Nutren® Fiber
Jevity® 1.2 Cal	Fibersource™ HN Ultracal® HN Plus	ProBalance®
Jevity® 1.5 Cal	Isosource® 1.5 Cal	(continued)

Oral/Enteral Nutrition Supplement Brand Equivalents

(continued)

ROSS	NOVARTIS	NESTLE
Promote®		Replete® NutriHeal™
Promote® with Fiber	Isosource® VHN Protain XL®	Replete® with Fiber
Glucerna®	Choice DM® Bev. Diabetisource® AC Resource® Diabetic	Glytrol®
Pulmocare®	Novasource® Pulmonary Respalor®	NutriVent®
Optimental®	Impact®	Peptamen®
Perative®	Impact® Plus Vivonex® Plus	Crucial® Peptamen®
Vital® HN	Criticare HN® Vivonex® T.E.N. Tolerex®	
Enlive!®	Boost Breeze® Resource® Fruit Bev.	NuBasics® Juice Drink

Nutrition Supplements by Indication (>6 years old only)

Indication		Comments
Normal Needs (1.0 kcal/mL)	Boost® (Novartis®)	
	Ensure® (Ross®)	
	Isosource® (Novartis®)	
	NuBasics® (Nestle®)	
	Resource® Standard (Novartis®)	
	Compleat® (Novartis®)	Blenderized whole food
	Nutren® (Nestle®)	
High Calorie (1.5 kcal/mL)	Boost Plus® (Novartis®)	
	Ensure Plus® (Ross®)	
	NuBasics® Plus (Nestle®)	
	Resource Plus® (Novartis®)	
	Isosource® 1.5 Kal (Novartis®)	0.8 g fiber per 100 mL
Very High Calorie (2.0 kcal/mL)	Hi-Cal™ (Ross®)	
	Resource® 2.0 (Novartis®)	
	VHC 2.25 (Nestle®)	2.25 kcal/mL
	TwoCal® HN (Ross®)	0.5 g fiber per 100 mL

(continued)

Nutrition Supplements by Indication (>6 years old only)

(continued)

Indication		Comments
Clear Liquid	Boost Breeze® (Novartis®)	Contains whey protein
	Enlive!® (Ross®)	
	NuBasics® Juice Drink (Nestle®)	
	Resource® Fruit Beverage (Novartis®)	
High Fiber	Boost® with Fiber (Novartis®)	1.1 g fiber per 100 mL
	Ensure® Fiber with FOS (Ross®)	To relieve diarrhea
	Fibersource™ (Novartis®)	1 g fiber per 100 mL
	Jevity® 1 Cal (Ross®)	1.44 g fiber per 100 mL
	Nutren® Fiber (Nestle®)	1.4 g fiber per 100 mL
	Ultracal® (Novartis®)	1.44 g fiber per 100 mL
	Jevity® 1.2 Cal (Ross®)	2.2 g fiber per 100 mL
	Jevity® 1.5 Cal (Ross®)	2.2 g fiber per 100 mL
Specialty Formulas	Nepro® (Ross®)	Patients on dialysis
	Oxepa® (Ross®)	Patients on ventilators
	Peptamen® (Nestle®)	Elemental
	Peptamen® 1.5 (Nestle®)	Elemental / high calorie
	Pulmacare® (Ross®)	Renal insufficiency/not on dialysis

Healthy Weight Guidelines

- A true healthy weight is determined by optimal functioning and appropriate vital signs, including blood pressure, body temperature, heart rate, cardiac output, reproductive functioning, and so on.
- A true healthy weight can be maintained without purging, excessive exercise or restrictive eating; this weight is maintained with appropriate eating behaviors and is accompanied by an adequate but not obsessive interest in food.
- There is no universal standard for determining healthy weight for adults.
- Always estimate healthy weight as a range (e.g. 110-120 pounds) rather than a fixed number, and explain to patients the limitations of weight estimates.
- Standard growth charts (see next page) can provide guidelines for children and teens less than 18 years of age. Plot current height for age and find the corresponding weight for age at the same percentile. This is useful as a suggested minimum weight. Obviously weight recommendations may need to be adjusted as height increases.
- Body mass index (BMI), body composition testing, and other standards for estimating healthy weight should not be used without clinical judgment and acceptance of these methods' limitations.
- Do not assume a patient's pre-eating disorder weight is his or her healthy weight without assessing childhood growth pattern and past weight history.

Standard Growth Chart for Girls 2-20 years of age

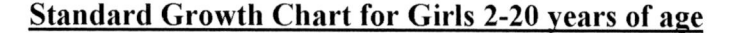

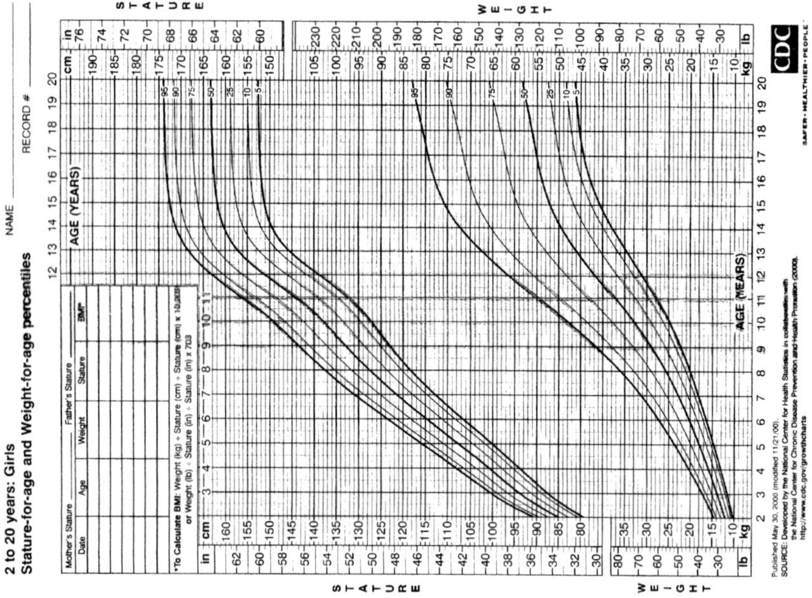

2 to 20 years: Girls
Stature-for-age and Weight-for-age percentiles
NAME
RECORD #
Mother's Stature
Father's Stature
Date
Age
Weight
Stature
BMI*
*To Calculate BMI: Weight (kg) ÷ Stature (cm) ÷ Stature (cm) x 10,000
or Weight (lb) ÷ Stature (in) ÷ Stature (in) x 703
AGE (YEARS)
STATURE
WEIGHT
in
cm
kg
lb
Published May 30, 2000 (modified 11/21/00).
SOURCE: Developed by the National Center for Health Statistics in collaboration with
the National Center for Chronic Disease Prevention and Health Promotion (2000).
http://www.cdc.gov/growthcharts
CDC
SAFER · HEALTHIER · PEOPLE™

Standard Growth Chart for Boys 2-20 years of age

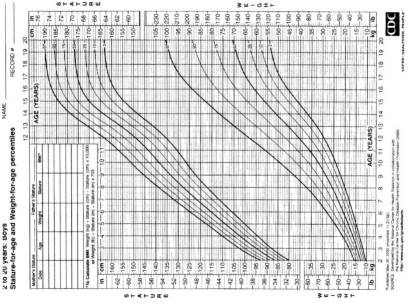

2 to 20 years: BOYS
Stature-for-age and Weight-for-age percentiles

NAME

RECORD #

Body Mass Index (BMI)

To calculate Body Mass Index (BMI):

$$\left(\frac{\text{Weight in kilograms}}{\text{Height in meters} \times \text{Height in meters}} \right)$$

~ OR ~

$$\left(\frac{\text{Weight in pounds}}{\text{Height in inches} \times \text{Height in inches}} \right) \times 703$$

Or use BMI nomogram (see next page)

Notes: Body Mass Index measurements do not differentiate between body fat mass and lean tissue mass (skeleton, muscle, water, etc.). A patient at a personal healthy weight may appear overweight or obese according to BMI standards. Body Mass Index Standards should not be applied to children, as early developing children may be inappropriately placed in the overweight or obese category.

Nomogram for Body Mass Index

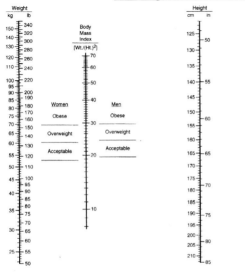

To use this nomogram, draw a line from the patient's weight on the far left axis to the patient's height on the far right axis. The line will cross the middle axis at the patient's BMI.

Source: The University of Texas Health Science Center at San Antonio. (2005 Edition). *Positively Aging®: Choices and Changes.* San Antonio, Texas, U.S.A. (Funded by the National Institutes of Health – Science Education Partnership Award, grant #R25-RR-18549 with National Center for Research Resources and National Institute on Aging). http://teachhealthk-12.uthscsa.edu.

Government Standards for Adult Body Mass Index (US only)

BMI	Weight Status
Below 18.5	Underweight
18.5 – 24.9	Normal
25.0 – 29.9	Overweight
30.0 and Above	Obese

Notes: Body Mass Index measurements do not differentiate between body fat mass and lean tissue mass (skeleton, muscle, water, etc.). A patient at a personal healthy weight may appear overweight or obese according to BMI standards. Body Mass Index Standards should not be applied to children, as early developing children may be inappropriately placed in the overweight or obese category.

Promoting Safe and Healthy Weight Gain

- Avoid discussing weight-related numbers with patients, including future weight goals, current weight, and weight increases. Patients may become obsessed with certain numbers, afraid of certain weights, and may sabotage treatment when nearing a "healthy" weight.
- Do not argue with a patient about goal weight or weight gain goals.
- In higher levels of care, such as a hospital or treatment center more rapid weight gain (up to 5 pounds per week for adults, 3 pounds per week for adolescents) can be expected and monitored. In outpatient care, weight gain may be slower and less consistent.
- Increase intake based on weight to promote weight gain of up no more than 5 pounds per week for adults, no more than 3 pounds per week for adolescents. Consistent small gains are preferred.
- One day of weight loss does not negate a pattern of weight gain and should not be considered a failure.
- Reassure patient that initial weight gain may be rehydration and repletion, not body fat, and that ultimately, health is the goal, not a particular weight.
- Weight restoration does not signify mental health or full physical recovery. Patients should continue care beyond weight restoration.

Promoting Safe and Healthy Weight Maintenance

- During the weight gain process, and particularly once patient has reached a healthy weight, encourage the purchase of appropriately sized clothes that fit, and encourage patient to donate/give away old clothes that are too small.
- When purchasing new clothes, it may be helpful to shop with a supportive friend or family member who will conceal size labels and remove them once clothes are purchased.
- Reassure patient that weight normally fluctuates day to day and even within one day. Discourage frequent weighing as this can cause unnecessary panic.
- Ideally patient should strive to weigh no more than one weight per week. Multiple caregivers should coordinate so that patient is not weighing on a variety of scales or more than once per week.
- Remind patient that sudden weight gain may be due to:
  - Food or beverages in stomach
  - Water retention
  - Constipation
  - Return of menses

  and does not require immediate compensatory action.
- Encourage patient and family members to strive for a weight neutral environment in the home/workplace, where eating, weight, and diets are not discussed.

Promoting Safe and Healthy Weight Loss

- Recommend weight loss to eating disordered patients at your own risk! For eating disordered patients, a medical mandate to lose weight can result in an increase in stress-related eating and therefore weight GAIN.
- If you choose to recommend weight loss, a referral to an appropriate nutrition professional is ESSENTIAL.
- Emphasize to patients that weight loss is acceptable as a **consequence** of healthy eating habits. It is not acceptable as a **goal** to be achieved at any cost.
- Do not overemphasize the importance of weight versus other vital signs, quality of life, and mental health.
- Remind patients that weight alone does not determine health.
- Remind patients that contrary to popular opinion, weight is not under conscious human control. It is a natural body function. The more we worry about it, the more our normal ability to eat is disrupted.
- Weight loss should be achieved through medical health, healthy eating, and healthy physical activity.
- Emphasize that many health parameters can be improved with improved nutrition and activity patterns even without observable weight loss. Physical fitness has been shown to be a better predictor of longevity than weight itself.

Estimating Daily Energy Expenditure

There is only one accurate way to measure daily energy expenditure: using a metabolic cart that measures one person's inhaled oxygen and exhaled carbon dioxide for 24 hours. Any other calculation must be considered an estimation, and must be used along with clinical judgment and health parameters to guide nutritional repletion and education. There are many equations used to estimate metabolic rate. One such equation follows, and must be used with the activity factors on the next page.

Men: $RMR = 10(wt) + 6.25(ht) - 5(age) + 5$

Women: $RMR = 10(wt) + 6.25(ht) - 5(age) - 161$

RMR = Resting Metabolic Rate
w = weight in kilograms
h = height in centimeters
age = age in years

Source: Mifflin MD et al. A new predictive equation for resting energy expenditure in healthy individuals. *Am J Clin Nutr.* 1990;51:241-247.

Estimating Total Daily Energy Expenditure

RMR x Activity Factor

Activity Factor	Activity Category
1.2	Bed Rest
1.3	Very Light
1.5	Light
1.6	Moderate
1.9	Heavy
2.2	Exceptional

Estimating Daily Energy Expenditure

Another method of estimating daily energy expenditure is to use a patient's current height to estimate how many calories they spend per 24 hours.

By Height: kcals/cm: 11-14 years old use 14 kcal/cm,
                                        15-18 years old use 13.5 kcal/cm

Body weight can also be used to estimate daily energy use, however current body weight can only provide current energy intake. To promote weight loss or gain, use a patient's standard or target body weight.

By Weight in kg: kcals/kg: 11-14 years old use 47 kcal/kg
                                        15-18 years old use 40 kcal/kg
                                        >18 years old use 30-35kcal/kg

By Weight in lbs: kcals/lb: 11-14 years old use 22-26 kcal/lb
                                        15-18 years old use 18-20 kcal/lb

Physical Activity Guidelines for All Eating Disorder Types

- Assess physical stability and health and/or seek guidance from patient's physician, physical therapist or exercise physiologist before recommending exercise.
- Educate patient about the energy cost of preferred activities, as well as the energy expended during non-exercise activities.
- If weight loss is contraindicated, modify meal plan to compensate for the energy cost of added activities.
- Exercise may be appropriate below a healthy weight, as long as patient is able to eat appropriately. Exercise is not appropriate below a healthy energy intake; if patient is unable to eat enough for activities of daily living, extra activities should not be allowed.
- Review with patient reasons to stop exercising immediately: chest pain, shortness of breath, dizziness, fatigue.
- Encourage patient to exercise at lower intensity, duration, and frequency than usual until physical response to exercise is observed.
- Competitive sports and previously compulsive activities should be discouraged at the beginning of recovery. Patients may find it difficult to respond to signs of fatigue when in competition.
- Encourage activities with a non-competitive, social, or meditative component.

Levels of Treatment for All Eating Disorder Types

- Outpatient Care – Individual appointments with care providers in an office or clinic setting.

- Intensive Outpatient Program – Group meetings supervised by care providers in 2-4 hour increments several times a week.

- Day Treatment – Daily groups and individual appointments during the working day/week.

- Partial Hospitalization – Full hospital care except patient sleeps at home.

- Inpatient Hospitalization – Full hospital care in either a medical, psychiatric, or eating disorders unit.

- Residential Treatment/Treatment Center – A freestanding treatment facility that may or may not be affiliated with a hospital. Treatment may be short- or long-term.

Referral Guidelines for Eating Disorders Level of Care

Characteristic	Level 1: Outpatient	Level 2: Intensive Outpatient	Level 3: Partial Hospitalization (Full-Day Outpatient Care)	Level 4: Residential Treatment Center	Level 5: Inpatient Hospitalization
Medical complications	Medically stable to the extent that more extensive medical monitoring, as defined in levels 4 and 5, is not required			Medically stable to the extent that intravenous fluids, nasogastric tube feedings, or multiple daily laboratory tests are not needed	For adults: heart rate <40 bpm; blood pressure <90/60 mm Hg; glucose <60 mg/dl; potassium <3 meq/liter; electrolyte imbalance; temperature <97.0 °F; dehydration; or hepatic, renal, or cardiovascular organ compromise requiring acute treatment. For children and adolescents: heart rate in the 40s; orthostatic blood pressure changes (>20-bpm increase in heart rate or >10-20-mm Hg drop); blood pressure below 80/50 mm Hg; hypokalemia or hypophosphatemia
Suicidality	No intent or plan			Possible plan but no intent	Intent and plan

(continued)

Characteristic	Level 1: Outpatient	Level 2: Intensive Outpatient	Level 3: Partial Hospitalization (Full-Day Outpatient Care)	Level 4: Residential Treatment Center	Level 5: Inpatient Hospitalization
Weight as % of healthy body weight (for children, use rate of weight loss)	>85%	>80%	>75%	<85%	<75% (for children and adolescents: acute weight decline with food refusal even if not <75% below healthy body weight)
Motivation to recover, including cooperativeness, insight, and ability to control obsessive thoughts	Fair to good	Fair	Partial; preoccupied with ego-syntonic thoughts more than 3 hours a day; cooperative	Poor to fair; preoccupied with ego-syntonic thoughts 4-6 hours a day; cooperative with highly structured treatment	Very poor to poor; preoccupied with ego-syntonic thoughts; uncooperative with treatment or cooperative only in highly structured environment
Comorbid disorders (substance abuse, depression, anxiety)	Presence of comorbid condition may influence choice of level of care				Any existing psychiatric disorder that would require hospitalization
Structure needed for eating/ gaining weight	Self-sufficient		Needs some structure to gain weight	Needs supervision at all meals or will restrict eating	Needs supervision during and after all meals or nasogastric/special feeding
Impairment and ability to care for self; ability to control exercise	Able to exercise for fitness, but able to control compulsive exercising		Structure required to prevent patient from compulsive exercising	Complete role impairment, cannot eat and gain weight by self; structure required to prevent patient from compulsive exercising	

(continued)

Referral Guidelines for Eating Disorders Level of Care

(continued)

Characteristic	Level 1: Outpatient	Level 2: Intensive Outpatient	Level 3: Partial Hospitalization (Full-Day Outpatient Care)	Level 4: Residential Treatment Center	Level 5: Inpatient Hospitalization
Purging behavior (laxatives and diuretics)	Can greatly reduce purging in non-structured settings; no significant medical complications such as ECG abnormalities or others suggesting the need for hospitalization			Can ask for and use support or use skills if desires to purge	Needs supervision during and after all meals and in bathrooms
Environmental stress	Others able to provide adequate emotional and practical support and structure		Others able to provide at least limited support and structure	Severe family conflict, problems, or absence so as unable to provide structured treatment in home, or lives alone without adequate support system	
Treatment availability/ living situation	Lives near treatment setting			Too distant to live at home	

Notes: [a] Adapted from La Via et al. (1).

[b] One or more items in a category should qualify the patient for a higher level of care. These are not absolutes, but guidelines requiring the judgment of physicians.

[c] Although this table lists percentages of healthy body weight in relation to suggested levels of care, these are only approximations and do not correspond to percentages based on standardized tables. For any given individual, differences in body build, body composition and other physiological variables may result in considerable differences as to what constitutes a healthy body weight in relation to "norms." For some, a healthy body weight may be 110% of "standard," whereas for others it may be 98%. Each individual's physiological differences must be assessed and appreciated.

Source: American Psychiatric Association. Reprinted with permission from the Diagnostic and Statistical Manual of Mental Disorders, Fourth Edition, Text Revision, Copyright 2000.

Outpatient Eating Disorder Treatment May Include:

- Dental Professional – For damage control/repair of teeth and oral health, especially in the cases of stress-related teeth grinding (bruxism) and chronic vomiting. Chronic malnutrition can also cause gum disease and loosening of teeth.
- Dietitian – For medical nutrition therapy (nutrition assessment and recommendations), and/or ongoing nutrition counseling.
- Family Therapist – To support patient in communicating and/or improving relationships with family members.
- Individual Therapist – May be a psychologist, nurse, nurse practitioner, social worker, professional counselor, guidance counselor, minister, rabbi, etc., to provide individual talk therapy, cognitive behavioral or dialectical behavioral therapy, social skills, and problem solving.
- Massage Therapy – For stress management and to provide a safe experience of the physical body.
- Meal Therapy – For practicing new or recovering eating behaviors (alone or with family members, friends, professionals or other patients) in a supportive environment.

(continued)

<u>Outpatient Eating Disorder Treatment May Include:</u>
<small>(continued)</small>

- Meditation – For relaxation/stress management and to learn to decrease impulsivity; to become more accepting of emotions.
- Occupational Therapist, Art Therapist – For emotional healing through creative expression and/or constructive activity.
- Physical Therapist, Exercise Physiologist, or other Movement Therapist – For exercise prescription and supervision, as well as physical activity designed for stress management and health rather than weight loss.
- Physician – May be an internist, family doctor, pediatrician, etc. to monitor physical health and treat symptoms as needed.
- Psychiatrist – For assessment and medical management as needed for symptoms such as depression, anxiety, obsessive thinking, compulsive behaviors, self-harm, insomnia, binge eating.
- Specialist Physician – Cardiologist, endocrinologist, gastroenterologist, gynecologist, etc. for more specific health assessment and needs
- Speech Pathologist – For evaluation of feeding/swallowing abilities.
- Support Group or Therapy Group – For moral support and group interaction and confrontation in a supervised environment.

Referral Guidelines for Nutrition Counseling with a Registered Dietitian

- Unexplained or rapid weight loss or weight gain; especially in adolescents.

- Repeated unsuccessful attempts to gain or lose weight.

- Poor health or poor growth due to poor nutrition.

- Prescription of a special diet for a nutrition-related illness.

- Picky eating or change in food preferences, such as vegetarianism.

- Harmful, restrictive, obsessive, or excessive eating or other eating issues.

- Fatigue or changes in athletic performance.

- Prescription of medication known to cause weight changes.

- Patient requests nutrition advice.

Role of the Dietitian in Eating Disorders Care

- Evaluate the diet and share with psychiatrist and other physicians nutrition information that may affect physical and mental health or medication needs.
- Construct a healthy eating pattern individualized to each patient to address current nutrition concerns and physical needs.
- Help patient establish this healthy eating pattern.
- Challenge food myths.
- Explain the role of proper nutrition and food in physical health.
- Identify disordered eating behaviors that interfere with proper nutrition.
- Discover and help resolve disordered thoughts and feelings around food, eating and body size.
- Refer information discovered about the underlying stress issues to the mental health therapist. Free the therapist from nutrition discussions.
- Offer active learning activities (when appropriate), such as cooking, eating, or grocery shopping, to help teach new behaviors and acceptance of food-related tasks and environments. Model appropriate eating in these situations.
- Communicate frequently with other members of the treatment team regarding nutrition interventions and patient's health status.

Referral Guidelines for Behavioral Counseling with a Mental Health Professional

- Relationship or family problems, such as divorce, death in the family, etc.
- Behavior changes as a result of stress or life events (eating, violence, substance abuse, not eating, not sleeping, excessive exercise, self-harm).
- Difficulty caring for self or children, difficulty with activities of daily living.
- Traumatic event(s), including diagnosis of severe, stigmatizing, or debilitating illness and medical recommendations that change quality of life, e.g. bed rest, chemotherapy, insulin shots.
- Depression, anxiety or other overwhelming emotions, whether reported or observed (crying in session, agitation, pacing, violence).
- Family member(s) are preoccupied with patient's weight or eating.
- Sudden change in behavior, mood, or mental state.
- Inability to change even though patient expresses that change is desired.
- Fears, anxiety, stress, whether warranted or unwarranted, about the course of the eating disorder and/or recovery.

Encouraging a Patient to Pursue Counseling

Some patients may hold an unwarranted stigma against mental health care, whether because of past experiences or simply stereotypical beliefs. Encourage your patient who needs counseling to consider an evaluation of a therapist as an interview, and to try more than one therapist if needed to find a good match. Other ways to encourage your patient to follow your recommendation include the following.

- Specify which issues require counseling (or "management").
- "I'm a good listener, but I don't think I'm the best person to give you advice."
- "I can see how hard you are working on this issue, and in my experience, when someone wants to change and can't, there is often an emotional component."
- Suggest one visit, at least to make contact.
- Set a pre-set limit - "If after 6 weeks, xyz has not happened, I will recommend that you see a counselor."
- "I have to insist that before we set our next appointment, you have at least one meeting with a counselor."

Glossary of Psychotherapy Terms Related to Eating Disorders

Transference: Transference is the experience of feelings, drives, attitudes, and defenses toward a person in the present that do not fit that person but are a repetition of reactions originating in childhood, unconsciously displaced onto figures in the present. Example: A college-age client begins to resist all of the nutritionist's ideas and behaves rebelliously just as she did with her parents when she was a teen.

Counter transference: Counter transference refers to the *therapist's* reactions to the client. There are two kinds of counter transference. The first is "our stuff" that could interfere with the therapy and needs to be addressed in supervision. Examples: The therapist on a limited budget feels jealous of a client who is wealthy. The therapist has been feeling unsuccessful and needs the next client to be doing well in order to confirm her competence. The other kind of counter transference refers to reality-based reactions to the client's behavior. These may be a source of insight into the client. Examples: Feelings of resentment can be a useful clue that the client is expecting too much and the therapist needs to ask for more responsibility. Boredom or sleepiness could mean the client is not connecting with you. They are probably skirting issues and on the surface with themselves too.

Obsession: Recurrent and persistent thoughts, impulses or images that go beyond worrying about life events. Example: A person thinks about food or their weight so much that it crowds out much of their other daily thoughts.

Compulsion: A recurrent behavior that a person feels driven to perform in response to an obsession or rigid rule. The behavior is aimed at avoiding some kind of distress, though the behavior is not directly related to the subject of the distress. Example: A person feels compelled to eat ice cream when feeling lonely.

(continued)

Glossary of Psychotherapy Terms Related to Eating Disorders

(continued)

Coping mechanism: A behavior or thought process used to lessen anxiety or the experience of stress. Coping is done deliberately and with at least a degree of consciousness. Example: Distracting oneself with a video game when nervous about flying.

Defense mechanism: An unconscious process that decreases anxiety caused by unacceptable thoughts or feelings. Unlike coping, defenses tend to be rigid and compelled and do not respond to conscious choice. Everyone uses defenses. Some are considered healthier than others. Each person favors a few defenses. There are at least 20 different defenses. Some of the more common ones are described here:

> **Altruism:** Healthy altruism becomes a defense when the satisfaction one obtains from helping others is used to obscure unacceptable feelings or conflict. Example: A person spends long hours volunteering at pet rescue work and so gets to avoid the pain of a recent relationship ending.

> **Asceticism:** This is the renunciation of certain pleasures in order to avoid the anxiety and conflict associated with gratifying impulses. This is often a defense in Anorexia Nervosa.

> **Compensation:** A person is compensating when trying to make up for perceived deficiencies. Example: The drive for academic or career success can be an effort to defend against feelings of worthlessness.

(continued)

Glossary of Psychotherapy Terms Related to Eating Disorders

Denial: A direct negation or refusal to accept aspects of reality that are painful. A certain amount of denial allows us to function, but it becomes more problematic the more it distorts reality. Examples: Denial about the inevitability of our death allows us to get on with life. A person may deny a diagnosis of diabetes to avoid uncomfortable feelings of vulnerability.

Intellectualization: This involves thinking and talking about feelings and impulses rather than feeling them. Example: A person can talk at length about a significant loss without experiencing any sadness.

Projection: The person attributes to others unacceptable thoughts and feelings that the person actually has but is not conscious of. Example: A client comes into a session and says, "You're going to hate me for this…"

Regression: The return to an earlier developmental stage or type of behavior in order to avoid present anxiety. It is quite obvious when it occurs in children. In adults it can simply look like a return to an easier time in their lives.

Repression: This involves keeping unwanted thoughts or feelings completely out of awareness. This is considered a relatively high-level defense. Example, a person has very little memory of her mother who died when she was 10 years old. By not remembering, she avoids the painful feelings of loss.

(continued)

Glossary of Psychotherapy Terms Related to Eating Disorders

(continued)

Somatization: The intolerable conflict is converted into physical symptoms. The person may also be preoccupied with symptoms as a substitute for attention to feelings.

Splitting: A person whose identity is poorly integrated will use this defense against anxiety by separating both their representation of themselves and others into all "good" or all "bad." These clients can be quite volatile and unpredictable because they are unable to maintain a constant, complex internal view of self and others. In treatment they may separate professionals on the treatment team into two dichotomous categories.

Personality Disorders: A category of mental health diagnosis that describe a pervasive pattern of behavior and experience of self that is significantly different than expected by the client's culture. The types of personality disorders include: paranoid, antisocial, borderline, histrionic, narcissistic, avoidant, dependent, and obsessive compulsive. The most common one in clients with eating problems is borderline personality disorder.

Substance Abuse: Regular use of a mind-altering substance to the extent that it adversely effects functioning.

Substance Dependence: Consistent use of a mind altering substance despite knowledge that it is causing a physical or psychological problem. Dependence includes development of a tolerance for larger and larger amounts to achieve the same effect and withdrawal symptoms if the substance is stopped.

Used by permission. Copyright 2003, Molly Kellogg. In <u>Moving Away from Diets:</u> Healing Eating Problems and Exercise Resistance, 2nd Edition, by Karin Kratina, Nancy L. King, and Dayle Hayes; Helm Publishing, 2003.

Factors to Consider When Matching a Patient to an Eating Disorder Treatment Center

Note: There are no right or wrong answers, only information.

- Does the facility accept patients who are medically unstable?
- Does the facility provide medical care/medical refeeding when indicated?
- What is the facility's philosophy of treatment/nutrition/eating disorders?
- Does the facility aid patients in finding follow-up care?
- What is the cost? What insurance coverage is available? Are payment plans available? Are charity beds available?
- What are criteria for discharge? What is the average length of stay?
- Is the facility only for patients with eating disorders or for all psychiatric care?
- Does the facility provide treatment for additional issues that patients may have, such as trauma, substance abuse or self-harm?
- Are visitors allowed? Do visitors/family members participate in treatment?
- Does the facility have a particular religious affiliation?
- Does the facility offer a step-down program or halfway house?

Find an Eating Disorders Treatment Professional, Facility or Support Group

Nationwide Nutrition Network - www.eatright.org/Public/index_7684.cfm
Eating Disorder Referral and Information Center - www.edreferral.com
National Association of Anorexia Nervosa and Associated Disorders - www.anad.org
National Eating Disorders Association - www.nationaleatingdisorders.org
Treatment Facilities index -- www.disordered-eating.com
HUGS International Inc. -- www.hugs.com
Healthtouch -- www.healthtouch.com
Overeaters Anonymous -- www.oa.com

Eating Disorders Professional Organizations & Conferences

International Association of Eating Disorder Professionals – www.iaedp.org
Academy of Eating Disorders -- www.aed.org
National Eating Disorders Organization -- www.nationaleatingdisorders.org
The Renfrew Center Foundation -- www.renfrew.org
Eating Disorders Coalition – www.eatingdisorderscoalition.org
Inner Escapes with Francie White -- www.innerescapes.com
Eating Disorders Boot Camp -- www.understandingnutrition.com
Counseling Intensive for Nutrition Therapists -- www.mollykellogg.com
Sports, Cardiovascular and Wellness Nutritionists Disordered Eating Subgroup –
    www.scandpg.org

Eating Disorder Advocacy Organizations

The Elisa Project – www.TheElisaProject.org
National Association of Anorexia Nervosa and Associated Disorders - www.anad.org
National Eating Disorders Association - www.nationaleatingdisorders.org
Eating Disorders Anonymous - www.eatingdisordersanonymous.org
Lifelines Foundation for Eating Disorders – www.lfed.org

Informational Eating Disorders Websites

Something Fishy - www.somethingfishy.org
Mirror Mirror - www.mirror-mirror.org
National Eating Disorder Screening Program - www.mentalhealthscreening.org
Gurze Books - www.bulimia.com
Anorexia and Related Disorders - www.anred.com
National Eating Disorder Information Centre (Canada) - www.nedic.ca
Eating Disorders Association of the United Kingdom - www.edauk.com
Lifelines Foundation for Eating Disorders – www.lfed.org
National Institute of Mental Health anorexia study - www.angenetics.org
Harvard Eating Disorders Center – www.HEDC.org

If you would like your treatment facility, website, or resource included in future editions of The Eating Disorder Pocket Guide, please let us know at info@understandingnutrition.com.

Bariatric Surgery and Eating Disorders

Many patients with eating disorders eventually become overweight or obese, and meet criteria for bariatric (weight loss) surgery. Regardless of the specific procedure performed, the goals of weight loss surgery are typically to reduce the capacity of a patient's stomach, to force malabsorption, and/or to provide negative feedback (in the form of nausea, vomiting, or diarrhea) when the recommended diet is violated.

Patients with eating disorders may find ways to "cheat" on their post-surgery diets, and may stop losing weight or even regain lost weight. No weight loss surgery can remove emotion-related eating patterns that have become ingrained. If a patient has used food as a medicating substance, the surgery either removes the "drug," revealing the underlying depression and/or anxiety; or fails to work when the patient finds ways around the restrictions.

Unfortunately, assessment for emotional eating, binge-eating disorder, bulimia, and/or an unhealthy relationship with food is not standardized in bariatric care. Eating disorders may be willfully hidden by a patient, or simply unrecognized by the patient and/or care providers. Because of the current popularity of bariatric surgeries, post-surgery patients with eating disorders are becoming more common.

Bariatric Surgery: General Postoperative Diet

Inpatient: Noncarbonated clear liquids (low sugar for Roux-en-Y gastric bypass [RYGB]) 30 cc every hour, increasing to every 15 minutes as tolerated; medicine cup on tray helpful for portion control.

Discharge (2 to 5 days – 4 weeks): High protein, low-fat full fluids advanced to pureed foods as tolerated (low sugar for RYGB); 5 – 6 small meals of 2 – 3 oz each.

4 to 8 weeks: Transition to regular diet. Semi-solids/soft low-fat foods as tolerated (low sugar for RYGB); 5 – 6 small meals of 2 oz each with protein supplements as needed.

8 weeks and on: regular textured low fat foods as tolerated (low sugar for RYGB); 5 small meals of 2 – 3 oz each with protein supplements as needed.

Maintenance: Balanced deficit diet with emphasis on lean proteins, vegetables, fruits, low-fat dairy, and whole grains; adequate hydration and micronutrient supplements; protein supplements as needed; 3 – 5 small meals per day; portion size usually no more than 4 – 6 oz per meal.

Reprinted, with permission, from SCAN'S PULSE, Spring 2005, Vol.24, No. 2, official publication of Sports, Cardiovascular, and Wellness Nutritionists (SCAN), American Dietetic Association, Chicago, IL.

Bariatric Surgery: Possible Food Intolerances

- Tough meat – beef or chicken and turkey

- Bread – when fresh or fluffy

- Rice, possibly pasta

- Fibrous / poorly digested vegetables – celery, mushrooms

- Fibrous parts of fruit – citrus membranes, skins

- Fried foods

- Added sugars

Reprinted, with permission, from SCAN'S PULSE, Spring 2005, Vol.24, No. 2, official publication of Sports, Cardiovascular, and Wellness Nutritionists (SCAN), American Dietetic Association, Chicago, IL.

Bariatric Surgery: Prohibited Eating Behaviors

The following may cause overeating, leading to pain, pressure, and/or involuntary vomiting:

- Eating or drinking too quickly

- Eating with distraction / stress

- Eating and drinking simultaneously

- Not chewing food adequately

- Ignoring satiety cues

- Drinking with a straw

- Carbonated beverages

Patients with eating disorders may be used to certain ways of eating and may require behavioral counseling in order to comply with their recommended diet. Many patients are unable to identify satiety cues or sit down to a meal without reading or watching television. Ideally these behaviors are addressed before surgery, but often they are not identified until later.

Reprinted, with permission, from SCAN'S PULSE, Spring 2005, Vol.24, No. 2, official publication of Sports, Cardiovascular, and Wellness Nutritionists (SCAN), American Dietetic Association, Chicago, IL.

Diabetes and Eating Disorders

Diabetes is often associated with eating disorders for several reasons.

- The diagnosis of diabetes, as well as its chronic nature and need for constant regulation, can lead to depression with associated lack of interest in food.

- The ongoing need to micromanage food and carbohydrate intake can lead to preoccupation with food, and/or the dichotomous labeling of foods as "good" or "bad."

- Rebellion against the chronic diagnosis and accompanying loss of independence and control can lead to maladaptive coping behaviors such as eating disorders.

- Excess insulin administration can cause a hypoglycemic reaction, which must be treated with oral intake of high-sugar foods. If this is a frequent occurrence, eventually it may lead to unwanted weight gain.

(continued)

Diabetes and Eating Disorders
(continued)

- Because hypoglycemia for someone with diabetes can be potentially life threatening, some patients choose not to administer adequate doses of insulin in an effort to prevent hypoglycemia. An additional side effect of inadequate insulin is weight loss via spilling glucose in the urine, which can cause permanent kidney damage. Patients with eating disorders may choose this dangerous weight control method in preference to long-term health.

- Dietary restrictions may increase deprivation-sensitive binge eating, with excessive exercise or inadequate insulin administration used as a purging method.

- Excessively restrictive eating and/or excessive exercise can be incorrectly believed to reverse the effects or even the diagnosis of diabetes.

Diabetes and Eating Disorders

The following patients may be at risk of diabetes-related complications:

- Patients with a history of anorexia, bulimia, binge eating, or compulsive exercise who are newly diagnosed with diabetes.

- Diabetes patients newly diagnosed with an eating disorder.

- Adolescent and pre-adolescent girls with Type I diabetes.

- Patients known to have diabetes who deny their diagnosis or refuse to comply with prescribed medication or diet.

- Eating disorder patients who become pregnant (studies show a higher risk of gestational diabetes in women with a past eating disorder diagnosis, regardless of how long they have been recovered).

- Patients with anxiety or obsessive compulsive tendencies and diabetes.

Diabetes and Eating Disorders Strategies

- All eating disorder patients who are obese should be checked for diabetes, since up to 50% of people with diabetes are undiagnosed.
- Binge eating should be assessed in all obese patients with diabetes, as irregular and excessive eating can cause irregularities and difficult management of blood glucose levels.
- Patients should be provided with supportive counseling to manage the stress of a chronic and lifestyle-altering diagnosis.
- Encourage patients to follow appropriate, not excessive, dietary guidelines for diabetes, i.e. a healthy, balanced diet, monitoring carbohydrate intake and incorporating low glycemic index foods. It is not necessary to eliminate sugar intake. Refer patients to a Registered Dietitian or Certified Diabetes Educator for dietary instruction and/or see www.eatright.org or www.diabetes.org for dietary guidelines.
- Individualize intervention to match patient needs.
- Evaluate metabolic parameters in addition to eating disorder progress, including Hemoglobin A1C, blood pressure, cholesterol, triglycerides, microalbumin, and so on.

Diabetes and Eating Disorders Recommendations

Adults with eating disorders and diabetes should be counseled to maintain their health parameters at the goal levels recommended by the American Diabetes Association for all adults with diabetes.

Glycemic control	
A1C	< 7.0%*
Preprandial capillary plasma glucose	90 – 130 mg/dl (5.0 – 7.2 mmol/l)
Peak postprandial capillary plasma glucose **	<180 mg/dl (<10.0mmol/l)
Blood pressure	<130/80 mmHg
Lipids	
LDL	<100 mg/dl (<2.6 mmol/l)
Triglycerides	<150 mg/dl (<1.7 mmol/l)
HDL	>40 mg/dl (>1.1 mmol/l)++

* Referenced to a nondiabetic range of 4.0—6.0% using a DCCT-based assay.
** Postprandial glucose measurements should be made 1-2 h after the beginning of the meal, generally peak levels in patients with diabetes.
+ Current NCEP/ATP III guidelines suggest that in patients with triglycerides ≥200 mg/dl, the "non0HDL cholesterol" (total cholesterol minus HDL) be used. The goal is ≤130 mg/dl.
++ For women, it has been suggested that the HDL goal be increased by 10 mg/dl.
Source: Copyright © 2005 American Diabetes Association from Diabetes Care, Vol. 28, Supplement 1, 2005;S4-S36. Reprinted with permission from The American Diabetes Association.

Diabetes and Eating Disorders Goals

- A1C is the primary target for glycemic control.
- Goals should be individualized.
- Certain populations (children, pregnant women and elderly) require special considerations.
- Less intensive glycemic goals may be indicated in patients with severe or frequent hypoglycemia.
- More stringent glycemic goals (i.e. a normal A1C, <6%) may further reduce complications at the cost of increased risk of hypoglycemia (particularly in those with type 1 diabetes).
- Postprandial glucose may be targeted if A1C goals are not met despite reaching preprandial glucose goals.

Note: Patients with diabetes will always need to be more occupied with food, during and after eating disorder recovery, than a patient without diabetes.

Source: Copyright © 2005 American Diabetes Association from Diabetes Care, Vol. 28, Supplement 1, 2005;S4-S36. Reprinted with permission from The American Diabetes Association.

Athletes and Eating Disorders

Although sports participation may increase self-esteem for many children and adults, athletes are still at risk of developing disordered eating, eating disorders, and for women, the Female Athlete Triad. Contributing factors include:

- Nutrition myths and misconceptions promoted by inexperienced coaching or training staff or spread among teammates, such as "Don't eat carbs after 6 p.m. or you'll get fat."
- Sports which traditionally encourage a specific body size and shape, such as ice dancing, figure skating, cheerleading, drill team, diving, horseback riding, and gymnastics.
- Sport-related weight requirements, including weight classes, weigh-ins, and team-wide body composition testing.
- Training or competition schedules that leave little time for eating adequately.
- Sport-specific misconceptions, such as "The leaner you are the faster you can run."
- Extreme thinking and the determination to pursue it, such as "If low-fat is good for you, then no fat is better."

(continued)

Athletes and Eating Disorders

(continued)

- General misconceptions about the human body, such as "If you still have your period, you're not training hard enough."
- Increasing portrayal of female athletes as sex symbols, with the associated pressure to meet unreasonable body shape ideals.
- A devastating or career-ending injury that is not grieved adequately or addressed appropriately by the athlete's support system.

Not all of these factors can be controlled or eliminated, and not all female athletes will develop eating disorders. Even when training at extreme levels, some female athletes can maintain menstruation and bone health by eating adequate calories to cover the energy cost of their sport.

Anyone working with female athletes should be aware of the risk factors and warning signs of eating disorders in order to promote appropriate eating and attitudes, to prevent as much disordered eating as possible, and to intervene when necessary.

Nutrition Guidelines for Athletes

- Eat a well-balanced and varied choice of foods most days.
- Try not to go more than 4 hours without eating, except when you are asleep, and eat something within 2 hours of waking up.
- Eat a carbohydrate snack 2 hours before exercise.
- Drink 1 cup (8 fluid ounces) of water 15 minutes before exercise and every 20 minutes during exercise.
- Replace each half pound lost during exercise with 1 cup of water.
- If exercise lasts more than 1 hour, a sports drink may be a better choice than water.
- Juice and soft drinks are not good choices for re-hydration.
- Eat a meal with carbohydrates and protein as soon as possible after exercise to re-supply stored energy in your body.
- Choose a good source of potassium every day - bananas and orange juice are examples.
- Choose a good source of iron every day - meat, peanut butter, and beans are examples.
- Maintain a healthy body weight - rapid weight loss weakens your muscles and endurance.

Low Carbohydrate Diets and Eating Disorders

"Low Carbohydrate" technically is a relative term that depends on needs, previous eating style, and relative amounts of other macronutrients (proteins and fats). However, in the past century, "low-carbohydrate" or "low-carb" has come to mean one of many fad diets, such as Atkins, South Beach and Sugar Busters, which restrict certain foods for at times unreasonable, and even untruthful, reasons.

Experience shows that most people who take up a low-carb diet return to their usual eating style (and usual weight) within a relatively short period of time. Eating disordered patients, however, are driven to maintain their diets, even in the face of physical decay and poor energy levels. It is indeed possible for someone with an eating disorder, particular if they have obsessive compulsive tendencies, to insist on a low-carb diet inappropriately (for example when they have been advised to gain weight by a doctor) and to often restrict themselves even further than even the diets recommend.

The rapid weight loss that patients initially experience and the good mood that ketosis provides are both confirmation, in the patient's mind, that "it's working." They don't realize that their muscle mass is being degraded to provide glucose. At the same time, they may develop an absolute fear of eating any carbs at all.

(continued)

<u>Low Carbohydrate Diets and Eating Disorders</u>
(continued)

Health care providers should be aware of the current fad diets in order to be prepared to deal with their backlash. Many of these diets are justified and/or promoted with a slogan such as "It's not a diet, it's a lifestyle!" We need to assess the misconceptions and address them with appropriate nutrition recommendations.

Possible reasons patients may "feel better" following a low carbohydrate diet:

- They may be paying attention to what they eat for the first time.
- They may be eating adequate protein for the first time.
- They may feel they are "accomplishing" something.
- They may be eating adequate fat for satiety and satisfaction for the first time.
- They feel the freedom of releasing their restrictions on favorite but previously "illegal" foods.
- They may feel less guilty after eating "on the plan."
- They may be eating regularly throughout the day and/or eating breakfast for the first time.
- They may be in ketosis, which can feel euphoric.
- They may be eating a normal amount of refined carbohydrates for the first time.
- They may be exercising for the first time.
- They may be losing weight.

(continued)

Low Carbohydrate Diets and Eating Disorders

(continued)

Diet authors usually only mention the positive effects of their diets. We need to educate our patients regarding the negative affects of low carbohydrate dieting.

- Loss of muscle mass to make glucose (with associated loss of metabolic power) due to inadequate energy intake.

- Excessive loss of water to flush out ketones leading to dehydration.

- Micronutrients usually provided with grains, vegetables, and fruits will be missing, and nutrient supplements cannot replace the natural benefits of real foods, such as phytochemicals that have not been named or identified yet.

- Inadequate fiber may cause constipation, higher lipids, or other gastrointestinal effects.

- Because of muscle loss, BMR will be lower and weight gain will be inevitable once usual eating style is resumed.

Preventing Eating Disorders in Children

1. Don't make disparaging comments on weight, body shapes, or what you or someone else is eating.

2. Throw away your bathroom scale and only weigh children at their medical check-ups.

3. Guide children to follow their own body's signals for when, what, and how much to eat. Teach them to say "No, thanks" to food that is offered when they're not hungry.

4. When a child or teen announces a decision to change their eating, always ask why. Listen for any ulterior motive that is not food-related, such as "So I'll have more friends," or "So I'll do better in school."

5. When a child you know is feeling down or disappointed, encourage healthy methods of expression, such as talking, writing or art, rather than eating or dieting.

6. Seek professional help for any child or teen who appears to be struggling with their weight, shape or eating. If needed, seek help for yourself in order to be a better role model.

Guidelines for Professionals Weighing Children

- Children should be weighed in private, apart from other children.

- Weight is just another vital sign, like your height, your heart rate, your blood pressure, or your temperature.

- Weight is something we monitor to see if you are healthy. But weight alone does not determine health.

- Weight is something you cannot control. It is a side effect of two things you can control: how much you eat, and how much you do. When you eat the right amount for you, your weight will be right for you, too.

- Weight changes are not something to celebrate or to be embarrassed of; they are a normal part of life.

NEVER make negative comments to children about their weight. NEVER make children think they have disappointed you or done something wrong because their weight is not what you expected. NEVER talk about your own weight issues in front of children. EVER.

Children's Food & Nutrition Books

Aaahh! School Lunch, by Molly Wigand & Mark Siegel
Bread and Jam for Frances, by Russell Hoban & Lillian Hoban
Bread, Bread, Bread, by Ann Morris
Come and Eat With Us, by Annie Kubler & Caroline Formby D.W.
The Picky Eater, by Marc Tolon Brown
Dining With Prunella, by Teddy Slater & Diane Dawson Hearn
Eat Up, Gemma, by Sarah Hayes & Jan Ormerod
Eating Fractions, by Bruce Mcmillan
Feast for 10, by Cathryn Falwell
I am Water, by Jean Marzollo
I Eat Dinner, by Margery Facklam & Anita Riggio
I'm a Seed, by Jean Marzollo
Its' Pumpkin Time, by Zoe Hall
Jamberry, by Bruce Degen Johnny
Appleseed, by Steven Kellogg
Little Brown Bear Does Not Want to Eat, by Claude Lebrun & Daniele Bour
Lunch, by Denise Fleming
No More Peas, Please!, by Anne Abernathy Roth & Lynn Armstrong Hirsch
Oliver's Vegetables, by Vivian French, Alison Barlett & Alison Bartlett
Peas and Honey: Recipes for Kids, by Kimberly Colen & Mandy Victor

(continued)

<u>Children's Food & Nutrition Books</u>
(continued)

Picky Nicky, by Cathy East Dubowski & Mark Dubowski
Pizza Party, by Grace Maccarone
Sack Lunch, by Bob Reese
So Hungry!, by Harriet Ziefert & Carol Nicklaus
The Berenstain Bears and Too Much Junk Food, by Stan Berenstain, et al
The Garden in Our Yard, by Grey Henry Quinn
The Hungry Little Boy, by Joan W. Blos & Dena Schutzer
The Little Mouse, the Ripe, Red Strawberry, and the Big Hungry Bear, by Don and Audry Wood
The Seven Silly Eaters, by Mary Ann Hoberman & Marla Frazee
The Tiny Seed, by Eric Carle
The Very Hungry Caterpillar, by Eric Carle
Today is Monday, by Eric Carle
Too Many Tamales, by Gary Soto
Two for Stew, by Barney Saltzberg (Contributor), et al
Uncle Willie and the Soup Kitchen, by Dyanne Disalvo-Ryan
Vegetables & Herbs, by Cecilia Fitzsimons
What Food Is This?, by Rosmarie Hausherr
Yoko, by Rosemary Wells
Zak's Lunch, by Martie Palatini, et al

Common Triggers of Eating Disorders

Many disparate factors have been known to trigger disordered eating behaviors for individuals with susceptible biology. The most significant common factor is an emotional incident or period in which adequate healthy outlets were not available for stress. Other commonly reported triggering incidents include:

- Intentional dieting to promote weight loss.

- Death or illness of a loved one, divorce or marriage (one's own or that of a close family member or friend), birth of a child, or other life-changing event.

- Rape, miscarriage, abortion, abuse, whether recent or recently recognized, trauma of any kind.

- Threats to safety or security, such as burglary, terrorism, mugging, or job loss.

- Moving to a new city, especially as a school-aged child; when the move is in response to a major life event; or when no one is known in the new location.

(continued)

Common Triggers of Eating Disorders

(continued)

- Disappointment, particularly social rejection.

- Comments about weight, size, or shape, either derogatory or complimentary; intentional or unintentional weight loss or gain of a family member.

- Mandated weight loss or gain for participation in sport, dance, or other activity.

To minimize risk of eating disorder development, provide other options to deal with stress. Any of the above is an appropriate indication for mental health counseling. We cannot prevent all eating disorders, but we can teach children more appropriate methods to cope with stress.

How to Answer Questions from Friends and Family/
How to Explain that a Loved One has an Eating Disorder

- Discuss with the patient how he/she would like the situation presented. If the patient is not comfortable with the diagnosis of eating disorder: "She's been having a hard time, but now she's getting help. Thanks for your concern."
- If the patient is comfortable with the diagnosis of eating disorder: "She's been struggling with an eating disorder, and now that we've recognized it, she's getting professional care. We'll keep you posted."
- If there is anything that the patient has requested for support, such as prayers, cards, or privacy, deliver these requests.

What Can We Do to Protect Our Other Children?

- STOP commenting on weight, body shapes, or what someone is eating.
- Guide children to follow internal body cues about what and how much to eat.
- Encourage healthy expression of feelings, not changing appearance, to feel better.
- If needed, seek help for your own eating issues.

Top 10 Reasons Not to Diet

1. Diets don't work. You lose weight and gain it right back (weight cycle), often regaining more than you lost.
2. Dieting is dangerous. It causes many deaths and injuries every year.
3. Diets are expensive and without value.
4. Dieting causes fatigue, lightheadedness, saps your energy and strength.
5. Dieting disrupts normal eating, causes bingeing, overeating and chaotic eating.
6. Dieting increases food preoccupation, so half your day or more is spent thinking about food and weight.
7. Dieting diminishes women, subverting their dreams and ambitions, keeping them playing the anticipation game. There's a lot more to life than this.
8. Dieting decreases self-esteem, feelings of well-being. Instead, accepting and respecting yourself as you are brings confidence, health and a sense of wellness and wholeness.
9. Dieting stunts mental and physical growth and development of young people.
10. Dieting increases size prejudice, makes people more judgmental and critical of themselves and others.

Reprinted from Women Afraid to Eat: Breaking Free in Today's Weight-Obsessed World, by Frances M. Berg. Copyright 1998. All rights reserved. Published by Healthy Weight Network, 402 South 14th Street, Hettinger, ND 58639 (701-567-2646; Fax 701-567-2602) website: www.healthyweight.net.

Books for Family Members & Friends

Your Dieting Daughter, by Carolyn Costin

Surviving an Eating Disorder: Strategies for Family & Friends, by Michelle Siegel

Intuitive Eating, by Evelyn Tribole and Elyse Resch

Secrets of Feeding a Healthy Family, by Ellyn Satter

How to Get Your Kid to Eat...But Not Too Much, by Ellyn Satter

Afraid to Eat: Children and Teens in Weight Crisis, by Francie Berg

You Count, Calories Don't, by Linda Omichinski

Making Weight: Healing Men's Conflicts with Food, Weight, and Shape, by Arnold Andersen, Leigh Cohn, and Thomas Holbrook

Body Wars, by Margo Maine

Father Hunger: Fathers, Daughters and Food, by Margo Maine

The Secret Language of Eating Disorders, by Peggy Claude-Pierre

Your Diet is Driving Me Crazy, by Cynthia Sass

The Golden Cage, by Hilde Bruch

When Your Child Has An Eating Disorder: A step-by-step workbook, by Abigail Natenshon

Anorexia Nervosa: A Survival Guide for Families, Friends, and Sufferers, by Janet Treasure

Eating Disorders: A Parent's Guide, by Rachel Bryant-Waugh & Bryan Lask

General Nutrition for Families

Meals Without Squeals: Childcare Feeding Guide and Cookbook, by Christine Berman
Child of Mine: Feeding With Love and Good Sense, by Ellyn Satter
How to Get Your Kid to Eat but Not Too Much, by Ellyn Satter
Secrets of Feeding a Healthy Family, by Ellyn Satter
Nutrition for Women, by Elizabeth Somer
Eating on the Run, by Evelyn Tribole
Intuitive Eating, by Evelyn Tribole and Elyse Resch
Stealth Health, by Evelyn Tribole
Like Mother, Like Daughter, by Debra Waterhouse

Books for Patients

Intuitive Eating, by Evelyn Tribole and Elyse Resch
The Beauty Myth, by Naomi Wolf
Body Wars, by Margo Maine
Hope, Help and Healing for Eating Disorders, by Greg Jantz
Full Lives, by Lindsay Hall
Making Weight: Healing Men's Conflicts with Food, Weight, and Shape, by Arnold Andersen, Leigh Cohn, and Thomas Holbrook

Books for Professionals

The Eating Disorder Source Book, by Carolyn Costin
Moving Away from Diets, by Karin Kratina, Dayle Hayes, and Nancy King
Counseling Tips for Nutrition Therapists, by Molly Kellogg
Intuitive Eating, by Evelyn Tribole and Elyse Resch

Books about Body Image

Bodylove: Learning to Like Our Looks-And Ourselves, by Rita Freedman
Body Traps: Breaking the Binds That Keep You from Feeling Good About Your Body, by Judith Rodin
Love the Body You Were Born With: A Ten-Step Workbook for Women, by Monica A. Dixon
Somebody to Love: A Guide to Loving the Body You Have, by Leslea Newman
Transforming Body Image: Learning to Love the Body You Have, by Marcia Hutchinson
What Do You See When You Look in the Mirror?: Helping Yourself to a Positive Body Image, by Thomas F. Cash
When Food is Love: Exploring the Relationship Between Eating and Intimacy, by Geneen Roth
Making Peace With Food: Freeing Yourself From the Diet/Weight Obsession, by S. Kano
It's Not About Food: Healing from the Obsession With Food and Weight, by Carol Normandi and Laurelee Roark
Emotional Weight: Change Your Relationship With Food by Changing Your Relationship With Yourself, by Colleen Sundermeyer

Water-Soluble Vitamins and Their Roles

Nutrient	Roles in Body	Deficiency	Toxicity	Sources
Thiamin Vitamin B1	Energy Metabolism, Appetite, Nerve Function	Beriberi - Weakness, Confusion, Heart Problems		In all foods, esp. pork products, liver, whole grains or enriched breads and cereals, legumes, nuts
Riboflavin Vitamin B2	Energy Metabolism, Vision, Skin	Ariboflavinosis - Cheilosis, Glossitis, Rash		Dairy products, meat, leafy greens, whole grains or enriched breads and cereals; destroyed by light
Niacin Vitamin B3 Nicotinic Acid Nicotinamide Niacinimide	Energy Metabolism, Skin, Nervous System, Digestive System	Pellagra - Diarrhea, Glossitis, Loss of Appetite, Weakness, Confusion	Diarrhea, Nausea, Vomiting, Dizziness, Flushing, Sweating	All protein-containing foods: Dairy, Eggs, Meat, Poultry, Fish, Breads and Cereals, Nuts *Can be made from the amino acid tryptophan.
Biotin	Energy Metabolism, Fat Synthesis, Amino Acid Metabolism, Glycogen Synthesis	Rare: Loss of Appetite, Nausea, Weakness, Dermatitis, Hair Loss		Widespread in foods and made by GI tract bacteria
Pantothenic Acid	Energy Metabolism	Rare: General Failure of Body Systems	Rare	Widespread in foods, esp. meats, fish, poultry, whole grains, and legumes

(continued)

Water-Soluble Vitamins and Their Roles

Nutrient	Roles in Body	Deficiency	Toxicity	Sources
Pyridoxine Vitamin B6 Pyridoxal Pyridoxamine	Amino Acid and Fatty Acid Metabolism, Tryptophan Conversion to Niacin, Red Blood Cells	Microcytic Anemia, Glossitis, Cheilosis, Dermatitis, Convulsions, Kidney Stones	Only with Supplementation: Nerve Damage, Fatigue	Green leafy vegetables, meats, fish, poultry, legumes, fruits, whole grains; lost when heated
Folic Acid Folacin Folate	DNA Synthesis, New Cell Formation	Megaloblastic Anemia, Diarrhea/Constipation, Glossitis, Confusion; Birth Defects		Leafy green vegetables, legumes, seeds, liver
Cobalamin Vitamin B12	New Cell Synthesis, Nerve Cells	Megaloblastic Anemia, Glossitis, Fatigue		All animal products; Vegans need a supplement
Vitamin C Ascorbic Acid	Collagen, Antioxidant, Amino Acid Metabolism, Immune System, Improves Iron Absorption	Scurvy: Anemia, Infections, Bleeding Gums, Muscle and Joint Pain, Rough Skin, Delayed Wound Healing	Cramping, Diarrhea, Headache, Insomnia, Kidney Stones	Citrus fruits, cabbage family, dark green vegetables, cantaloupe, strawberries, peppers, lettuce, tomatoes, potatoes, papayas, mangoes

Fat-Soluble Vitamins and Their Roles

Nutrient	Roles in Body	Deficiency	Toxicity	Sources
Vitamin A Retinol Retinoic Acid	Vision, Mucous Membranes and Skin, Bones and Teeth, Reproduction Immunity	Hypovitaminosis A: Joint Pain, Teeth Cracks, Anemia, Dehydration, Xerosis, Night Blindness, Hyperkeratosis	Hypervitaminosis A: Joint Pain, Headaches, Amenorrhea	Fortified Dairy Products and Margarine, Eggs, Liver; Beta-Carotene in spinach and leafy greens
Vitamin D Calciferol Cholecalciferol	Helps calcium and phosphorous build bones	Rickets, Osteomalacia: Misshapen legs, Deformed bones and teeth, Soft Bones	Hypervitaminosis D: Loss of appetite, kidney stones, tissue calcification	Made from cholesterol and sunlight; fortified milk and margarine, egg yolk, liver, fatty fish
Vitamin E Tocopherol Alpha-tocopherol	Antioxidant, protects cell membranes, fatty acids, and vitamin A	Hemolysis, Anemia, Weakness	Rare - only with supplementation - GI disturbance	Polyunsaturated plant oils incl. margarine, green leafy vegetables, liver, egg yolks, nuts, seeds, wheat germ, whole grains
Vitamin K Phylloquinone Napthoquinone	Helps make proteins that clot blood and regulate blood Ca	Hemorrhaging	Rare - only with supplementation - brain damage	Made by GI bacteria; liver, green leafy vegetables, cabbage family, milk

Food Sources of Vitamins by Vitamin

Fats, Oils & Sweets:
E = sunflower oil, safflower oil,
    cottonseed oil

Milk, Yogurt & Cheese Group:
A = fortified milk
B_2 = milk, cheese
B_{12} = milk, milk products
D = fortified milk

Vegetable Group:
A = carrots, sweet potatoes, leafy greens
C = broccoli, tomatoes, sweet peppers
    potatoes, sweet potatoes, leafy greens
Folate = leafy greens, broccoli
K = green tea, leafy greens, broccoli,
    brussels sprouts

Bread, Cereal, Rice & Pasta Group:
B_1 = wheat germ, whole grains, enriched
breads and cereals
B_2 = enriched breads and cereals
B_6 = whole-grain cereals

**_Meat, Poultry, Fish, Dry Beans
Eggs & Nuts Group:_**
A = liver, eggs
B_1 = legumes, beef liver, pork
B_2 = poultry, organ meat
B_6 = chickpeas, fish, poultry, meat
B_{12} = meat, eggs, fish
E = nuts, seeds
Folate = legumes, liver

Fruit Group:
A = apricots, cantaloupe, mango, peaches,
    watermelon
B_6 = avocados, bananas, watermelon
C = strawberries, kiwi, oranges, grapefruit
    cantaloupe
Folate = oranges, avocados   (continued)

E = wheat germ
Folate = fortified grains, whole grains
K = cereals, whole grains
Niacin = whole wheat bread, enriched cereals

Source: NCR-540-W Vitamins and Minerals in the Food Guide Pyramid, William D. Evers. Reprinted with permission from Purdue Cooperative Extension out of the Department of Foods and Nutrition.

Food Sources of Minerals by Mineral

Fats, Oils & Sweets:
Magnesium = chocolate

Milk, Yogurt & Cheese Group:
Calcium = milk, cheese, yogurt
Iodine = milk, cheese
Potassium = milk, milk products

Vegetable Group:
Calcium = Chinese cabbage, turnip greens, kale
Iodine = potatoes
Iron = spinach, potatoes, chard
Magnesium = leafy greens
Potassium = chard, spinach, potatoes, tomatoes, sweet potatoes

Bread, Cereal, Rice & Pasta Group:
Chromium = whole grains
Copper = whole grains
Iodine = cereals, crackers
Iron = whole grains, enriched breads, wheat germ

Meat, Poultry, Fish, Dry Beans
Eggs & Nuts Group:
Calcium = tofu, canned fish
Chromium = meats
Copper = liver, nuts, shellfish
Iodine = seafood, meat, eggs
Iron = red meat, legumes
Magnesium = nuts, legumes
Potassium = legumes, meats
Selenium = meat, seafood, fish, nuts, eggs
Zinc = meat, soybeans, oysters

Fruit Group:
Iron = dried fruit
Potassium = avocados, bananas, dried fruit

Magnesium = wheat germ
Potassium = whole-grain cereal
Selenium = bran, whole grains, wheat germ
Zinc = wheat bran, wheat germ, whole grains

Source: NCR-540-W Vitamins and Minerals in the Food Guide Pyramid, William D. Evers. Reprinted with permission from Purdue Cooperative Extension out of the Department of Foods and Nutrition.

Food Sources of Vitamins and Minerals by Food Group

Fats, Oils & Sweets:
E
Magnesium

Milk, Yogurt & Cheese Group:
A, B_2, B_{12}, D
Calcium, Iodine, Potassium

Vegetable Group:
A, C, Folate, K
Calcium, Iodine, Iron,
Magnesium, Potassium

Fruit Group
A, B_6, C, Folate
Iron, Potassium

Meat, Poultry, Fish, Dry Beans
Eggs & Nuts Group:
A, B_1, B_2, B_6, B_{12}, E, Folate
Calcium, Chromium, Copper,
Iodine, Iron, Magnesium,
Potassium, Selenium, Zinc

Bread, Cereal, Rice & Pasta Group:
B_1, B_2, B_6, E, Folate, K, Niacin
Chromium, Copper, Iodine, Iron,
Magnesium, Potassium, Selenium,
Zinc

Source: NCR-540-W Vitamins and Minerals in the Food Guide Pyramid, William D. Evers. Reprinted with permission from Purdue Cooperative Extension out of the Department of Foods and Nutrition.

Definitions of Dietary Reference Intakes (DRIs)

In 1997, the Food and Nutrition Board of the National Academy of Sciences revised the Recommended Dietary Allowances (RDAs) and created a new family of nutrient reference values – the Dietary Reference Intakes (DRIs). There are four types of DRI reference values:

1. **Recommended Dietary Allowance (RDA):** the average daily dietary intake that is sufficient to meet the nutrient requirement of nearly all (97 to 98 percent) healthy individuals in a particular group according to stage of life and gender.
2. **Adequate Intake (AI):** a recommended intake value based on observed or experimentally determined approximations or estimates of nutrient intake by a group (or groups) of healthy people that are assumed to be adequate; AI is used when an RDA cannot be determined.
3. **Tolerable Upper Intake Level (UL):** the highest daily nutrient intake that is likely to pose no risk of adverse health effects for almost all individuals in the general population. As the intake increases above the UL, the potential risk of adverse effects increases.
4. **Estimated Average Requirement (EAR):** a daily nutrient intake value that is estimated to meet the requirements of half the healthy individuals in a group according to life stage and gender – used to assess dietary adequacy and as the basis for the RDA.

Source: *Dietary Reference Intakes: The Story Continues*, International Food Information Council. Reprinted with permission from the IFIC Foundation, Washington, DC.

Legal Definitions of Food Label Nutrition Claims (US only)

Calories	
Calorie Free	Less than 5 calories per reference amount and per labeled serving
Low Calorie	40 calories or less per serving (and per 50 g if reference amount is small)
Reduced Calorie/ Less Calories	At least 25% fewer calories per reference amount than the reference food
"Light" or "Lite"	One-third fewer calories or 50% less fat per reference amount

Fat	
Fat Free	Less than 0.5 g of fat per reference amount and per labeled serving
Low Fat	3 g or less fat per reference amount (and per 50 g if reference amount is small)
Reduced /Less Fat	At least 25% less fat per reference amount than the reference food
% Fat Free	OK if meets the requirements for "Low Fat"; 100% Fat Free must be "Fat Free"

(continued)

Legal Definitions of Food Label Nutrition Claims (US only)

Saturated Fat	
Saturated Fat Free	Less than 0.5 g saturated fat and less than 0.5 g trans fatty acids per reference amount and per labeled serving
Low Saturated Fat	1 g or less per reference amount and 15% or less of calories from saturated fat
Reduced/Less Saturated Fat	At least 25% less saturated fat per reference amount than an appropriate reference food (reference food may not be "Low Saturated Fat")

Cholesterol	
Cholesterol Free	Less than 2 mg per reference amount and per labeled serving (contains no ingredient that contains cholesterol except as noted by an asterisk)
Low Cholesterol	20 mg or less per reference amount (and per 50 g of food if reference amount is small)
Reduced/Less Cholesterol	At least 25% less cholesterol per reference amount than an appropriate reference food (reference food may not be "Low Cholesterol")
	Cholesterol claims are only allowed when food contains 2 g or less of saturated fat per reference amount

(continued)

Legal Definitions of Food Label Nutrition Claims (US only)

Sodium	
Sodium Free	Less than 5 mg per reference amount and per labeled serving (contains no ingredient that is sodium chloride or generally understood to contain sodium except as noted by an asterisk)
Low Sodium	140 mg or less per reference amount (and per 50 g if reference amount is small)
Reduced / Less Sodium	At least 25% less sodium per reference amount than an appropriate reference food (reference food may not be "Low Sodium")
Salt Free	Must meet the criterion for "Sodium Free"
No Added Salt / Unsalted	No salt added during processing; must declare "This is Not A Sodium Free Food" on information panel if food is not "Sodium Free"
Lightly Salted	50% less sodium than normally added to reference food and in not "Low Sodium", so labeled on information panel

(continued)

Legal Definitions of Food Label Nutrition Claims (US only)

Sugar	
Sugar Free	Less than 0.5 g sugars per reference amount and per labeled serving (contains no ingredient that is a sugar or generally understood to contain sugars except as noted by an asterisk)
Low Sugar	Not defined; no basis for recommended intake
Reduced/Less Sugar	At least 25% less sugars per reference amount than an appropriate reference food
No Added Sugars / Without Added Sugar	Allowed if no sugar or sugar containing ingredient is added during processing; must state if food is not "Low" or "Reduced Calorie"

Source: US Food and Drug Administration, *A Food Labeling Guide – Appendix A*

Legal Definitions of Food Label Nutrition Claims (US only)

Relative Claims	
"Light" or "Lite"	No specific nutrient claim
"Lean"	On seafood or game meat that contains less than 10 g total fat, 4.5 g or less saturated fat and less than 95 mg cholesterol per reference amount and per 100 g
"Extra Lean"	On seafood or game meat that contains less than 5 g total fat, 2 g or less saturated fat and less than 95 mg cholesterol per reference amount and per 100 g
"High" or "Rich In" or "Excellent Source Of"	Contains 20% or more of the Daily Value (DV) of a nutrient
"Good Source of", "Contains" or "Provides"	Contains 10% -- 19% of the Daily Value (DV) for a nutrient
"More", "Added", "Extra" or "Plus"	Contains an additional 10% or more of the Daily Value (DV) for a nutrient

Source: US Food and Drug Administration, *A Food Labeling Guide – Appendix B*

Iron Levels in Common Foods

Women need 15 mg each day.
Men need 12 mg each day.

Amount of Iron	Food Source
8.0 mg	½ C Cream of Wheat or Malt-O-Meal
5.0 mg	2 oz. Beef liver 1 C enriched ready-to-eat breakfast cereal
3.0 mg	4 oz. Steak or ground beef ½ C raisins ½ C cooked cereal (oatmeal, grits, bran) ¾ oz. Pumpkin seeds 1 T. molasses
2.0 mg	½ C pork and beans ¾ C cooked dark leafy greens or asparagus 1 C raw dark leafy greens ½ C cooked dried beans or split peas 3 oz. shellfish 3 oz. ham ¼ C soy nuts
1.0 mg	3 oz. cooked chicken, turkey, or pork 1 oz. pretzels ½ C enriched rice
0.7 mg	3 oz. canned salmon 1 egg yolk
0.5 mg	1 slice whole grain or enriched bread ½ C fruit or vegetable (x dark leafy greens) 1 T peanut butter 3 dried prunes or apricot halves

Note: The iron type found in meat, poultry, and fish is more efficiently absorbed than the iron in plants. Including a vitamin C source when eating plant sources of iron, such as a citrus fruit or juice, tomato, mango, bell pepper, potato, strawberries, broccoli, cabbage, or cantaloupe, can increase the bioavailability of iron.

Caffeine Levels in Common Foods and Beverages

Starbucks Espresso	320 mg per 16 ounces
Starbucks House Blend	220-564 mg per 16 ounces
No Doz, Vivarin	200 mg per tablet
Drip Brewed Coffee	85-150 mg per 8 ounces
Excedrin	130 mg per dose (2 tablets)
Jolt	72 mg per 12 ounce can
Haagen-Dazs Coffee Ice Cream	58 per Cup
Mountain Dew	52 mg per 12 ounce can
Snapple Iced Tea	42 mg per 16 ounce bottle
Dr. Pepper	40 mg per 12 ounce can
Colas	30-46 mg per 12 ounce can
Decaffeinated Coffee	Up to 22 mg per 16 ounces
Tea	20-90 mg per 5 ounces
Arizona Iced Tea	15-30 per 16 ounce bottle
Dark Chocolate	5-35 mg per ounce
Diet Colas	2-58 mg per can
Chocolate Milk	2-7 mg per 8 ounces
Milk Chocolate	1-15 mg per ounce
Herbal Tea	0

<u>Simple Snack Suggestions with Protein</u>

½ peanut butter & jelly sandwich & milk
Yogurt & ½ bagel
Apple & peanut butter
Cheese sandwich with lettuce & tomato
2 large hard pretzels & string cheese
Oatmeal cookies & milk
Saltines & veggie beef soup or cream soup
Graham crackers & milk
1 slice angel food cake & milk
Fruit & cottage cheese or yogurt
Oatmeal & milk
Applesauce & slice of cheese
Yogurt & fruit
Mini bagel pizzas
Cereal & Milk
Raisins & nuts or trail mix
Cottage cheese with canned fruit
Toaster-style blueberry waffle & milk
Goldfish® crackers & hard boiled egg
Cheese wedges & V8® juice
English muffin mini-pizza with 1 Tbsp tomato sauce & 1 slice of cheese
3 Oreo® cookies & milk
3 Fig Newtons® & milk
Rice Krispie® treat & peanut butter

Measurement Equivalent Conversions

LENGTH
****

To Find	Multiply by	When You Know
Inches	0.04	millimeters
Inches	0.4	centimeters
Feet	3.3	meters
Centimeters	2.54	inches

WEIGHT
****

To Find	Multiply by	When You Know
Ounces	0.035	grams
Pounds	2.2	kilograms
Grams	28	ounces
Kilograms	0.45	pounds

VOLUME
****

To Find	Multiply by	When You Know
Teaspoons	0.2	milliliters
Tablespoons	0.07	milliliters
Fluid Ounces	0.03	milliliters
Cups	4.23	liters
Milliliters	5	teaspoons
Milliliters	15	tablespoons
Milliliters	30	fluid ounces

<u>Weight & Measurement Equivalents</u>

Weight
1 pound (lb) = 16 ounces (oz)
1 kilogram (kg) = 2.2 pounds (lb)
1 ounce (oz) = 28.35 grams (g)
1 gram (g) = 0.035 ounce (oz)

Length
1 inch (in) = 2.54 centimeters (cm)

Prefix	Multiple of 10	Comparison
kilo (k)	1000	1 kilometer (km) = 1000 meters (m)
deci (d)	0.1	1 liter (L) = 10 deciliter (dL)
centi (c)	0.01	1 meter = 100 centimeters
milli (m)	0.001	1 liter (L) = 1000 milliliters (mL)
micro (μ)	0.000001	1 liter (L) = 1 million microliters (μ)

Volume Equivalents

1 tsp	= ⅓ Tbsp	= ¹⁄₆ fl oz	= 4.9 ml	(often rounded to 5 ml)
3 tsp	= 1 Tbsp	= ½ fl oz	= 14.8 ml	(often rounded to 15 ml)
2 Tbsp	= ⅛ cup	= 1 fl oz	= 29.6 ml	(often rounded to 30 ml)
4 Tbsp	= ¼ cup	= 2 fl oz	= 59.1 ml	(often rounded to 60 ml)
5⅓ Tbsp	= ⅓ cup	= 2 ⅔ fl oz	= 78.9 ml	(often rounded to 80 ml)
8 Tbsp	= ½ cup	= 4 fl oz	= 118.3 ml	(often rounded to 120 ml)
10⅔ Tbsp	= ⅔ cup	= 5 ⅛ fl oz	= 157.7 ml	(often rounded to 160 ml)
12 Tbsp	= ¾ cup	= 6 fl oz	= 177.4 ml	(often rounded to 180 ml)
14 Tbsp	= ⅞ cup	= 7 fl oz	= 207.0 ml	(often rounded to 210 ml)
16 Tbsp	= 1 cup	= 8 fl oz	= 236.6 ml	(often rounded to 240 ml)

1 tablespoon (T) = ½ fl oz = 3 teaspoons (t)
1 cup (C)= 8 fl oz = 16 tablespoons (T)
1 pint (pt) = 16 fluid ounces (fl oz)
1 quart (qt) = 32 fluid ounces (fl oz)
1 gallon (gal) = 4 quarts (qt)
1 liter (L) = 1,000 milliliters (mL)

Autobiography in Five Short Chapters
by Portia Nelson

Chapter I
I walk down the street.
There is a deep hole on the sidewalk.
I fall in. I am lost. I am helpless.
It isn't my fault.
It takes forever to find a way out.

Chapter II
I walk down the same street.
There is a deep hole on the sidewalk.
I pretend I don't see it.
I fall in again. I can't believe I am in
the same place, but it isn't my fault.
It still takes a long time to get out.

Chapter III
I walk down the same street.
There is a deep hole in the sidewalk.
I see it there. I still fall in, it's a habit.
My eyes are open.
I know where I am. It is my fault.
I get out immediately.

Chapter IV
I walk down the same street.
There is a deep hole in the sidewalk.
I walk around it.

Chapter V
I walk down another street.

To order additional copies of The Eating Disorders Clinical Pocket Guide, visit www.understandingnutrition.com, call 214-503-7100, or mail this order form to Understanding Nutrition, 6510 Abrams Road, Suite 302, Dallas, Texas, USA, 75231 with your check, money order (US dollars only) or credit card information.

Name: _____

Mailing Address: _____

_____

Phone Number: _____   Email: _____

1-9 copies: $32.95 each   10-20 copies: $29.95 each   Please contact us for orders over 20 copies.
Shipping: $2 per copy   Texas residents only: Add 8.25% sales tax

Number of Books: _____ x Rate = _____ + Tax_____ + Shipping_____ = Total: _____

Payment Method: __ Check (payable to Understanding Nutrition, PC) __ Money Order

__ Visa   __ MasterCard   __ American Express Number: _____

Last three numbers from back of card_____ or four numbers from front of card for American Express
For credit card orders only: Billing zip code if different from mailing address_____

Signature _____

About the Author

Jessica Setnick, MS, RD/LD, is a Registered Dietitian renowned for her work in the eating disorders field, both as a caregiver for patients and a teacher for other health professionals. Jessica is the founder of *Eating Disorders Boot Camp*, a 9-hour training workshop for professionals, and the corresponding home-study course. Jessica has co-authored a series of books with Shannon Purtell and Kelly Coutee - *The Eating Disorders Book of Hope and Healing*, *The Survivor's Book of Hope and Healing*, and *The Working Woman's Book of Hope and Healing*. For more information about these publications or a schedule of upcoming Eating Disorders Boot Camps (and companion workshop Molly Kellogg's Counseling Intensive), visit www.understandingnutrition.com, email info@understandingnutrition.com, or call (US) 214-503-7100.

The author would like to acknowledge all those who helped in the production of this work, particularly Tracy Siravo, Celena Torres, Gregory Schon, Merritt Olsen, and Barry Knezek. This guide is dedicated to my many patients, past, current and future; to everyone who works to eradicate, ameliorate and prevent the spread of this eating disorders crisis; and to those who simply provide what we all need most – relief and compassion for human suffering.